COMING TO AMERICA

JEWISH
AMERICANS

COMING TO AMERICA

JEWISH AMERICANS

ROBERT STEIN

Series editor: Barry Moreno

First edition for the United States, its territories
and dependencies, and Canada published in 2003
by Barron's Educational Series, Inc.

Copyright © 2002 by
THE IVY PRESS LIMITED

This book was created by
The Ivy Press Ltd., The Old Candlemakers, Lewes, East Sussex BN7 2NZ, UK

Creative Director Peter Bridgewater

Publisher Sophie Collins

Editorial Director Steve Luck

Design Manager Tony Seddon

Designer Andrew Milne

Senior Project Editor Caroline Earle

Editor Stephanie Schwartz-Driver

Picture Researcher Vanessa Fletcher

All inquiries should be addressed to:
Barron's Educational Series, Inc.
250 Wireless Blvd.
Hauppauge, NY 11788
www.barronseduc.com
International Standard Book No.: 0-7641-5626-8
Library of Congress Catalog No.: 2002108727
Printed and bound in China by Hong Kong Graphics and Printing Ltd
9 8 7 6 5 4 3 2 1

CONTENTS

COMING TO AMERICA

American-Jewish history has been characterized by three waves of immigrants from three different parts of the world. Although they shared a common religion, each group had a distinct cultural heritage that shaped their experience in the New World.

The great majority of American Jews today are of Ashkenazi descent, with their roots in central and eastern Europe and speaking Yiddish, a German dialect written in Hebrew. However, the first Jews to settle in North America were Sephardic. They originated in Latin countries and spoke Ladino, a combination of Spanish and Portuguese written in Hebrew letters. In fact, the few Ashkenazim to arrive in the early days assimilated into Sephardic traditions, and this trend was not to change until the early nineteenth century.

In 1492, the same year Columbus arrived in the Americas (with six Jews on board), Jews were expelled from Spain as part of the Spanish Inquisition. In search of a new home and religious freedom, many traveled to the New World, settling in the Spanish and Portuguese colonies in South America. Once the Inquisition spread across the Atlantic, however, they were forced to move on again, and in 1654, 22 Spanish-Portuguese (Sephardic) Jews, along with one Ashkenazi Jew,

all uprooted from Recife, Brazil, arrived in New Amsterdam. The environment they found there was scarcely hospitable. The Dutch governor at the time, Peter Stuyvesant, refused to admit these penniless Jews. It was not until the colony's governing board in Amsterdam forced the issue that the Jews were allowed to stay in the colony. In 1655, more Sephardic Jews arrived from Spain via Holland, again escaping the Inquisition.

שפיר וועט געווינען דיא קריעג!

אהר קומט אהער צו געפינען פרייהייט.
יעצט מוזם איהר העלפען דיא צו בעשיצען.
מיר מוזען דיא עלליים פערוואָרגען מים ווײַן.
לאזם חיי זאר נים גיין אין נויט

Nine years later, the British won New Amsterdam —which would soon become New York —in the Dutch Wars. Under the terms of the Treaty of Breda (1667), Britain guaranteed full rights of worship, trade, and individual property for all former Dutch subjects in the colony, Jews included. Despite the liberalism of this treaty, nearly all the original Jews left the colony before the English took over. The one exception was Asser Levy, the lone Ashkenazi of the original 23. Levy was to become the colony's first kosher butcher and a prosperous and respected citizen under the rule of Great Britain. He was probably the first Jew to own real estate in New York. For many years New York remained more welcoming to Jews than other British colonies, such as Puritan New England or Catholic Maryland. This made New York the early focus of Jewish immigration for many years.

BELOW: *When the British won New Amsterdam in 1664, they extended equal rights to Jewish immigrants.*

LEFT: *This 1918 poster, "Food Will Win the War," was designed to encourage Jewish-American immigrants to support the war effort.*

RIGHT: *The New Amsterdam colony (later to become New York) did not welcome the Sephardic Jewish immigrants who sought refuge there.*

EARLY COMMUNITIES

In colonial times, Jews settled along the Atlantic coast and in several southern colonies. During the seventeenth century, Rhode Island was the only New England colony that allowed a permanent Jewish community. That settlement was in Newport, where the Touro Synagogue, built in 1773, still stands as a memorial to the patriot and philanthropist Judah Touro. The son of a rabbi, Touro made his money in the import trade, and when he passed away in 1758, a bachelor, he left a fortune well in excess of $1 million. Other early Spanish-Portuguese Jewish communities were established in Charleston, South Carolina, and Savannah, Georgia. A Philadelphia congregation (Congregation Mikveh Israel) was organized about 1745. A Richmond community was established after the Revolution.

From the mid-nineteenth century onward, German Jews began arriving in the United States in large numbers. Coming out of an assimilated, emancipated background, many of them were well-educated but had been barred from many professions, from land-ownership, and even from marriage, and were dependent on costly letters of protection from provisional governments. On this side of the Atlantic, however, the German Jews were often indistinguishable from their fellow Germans.

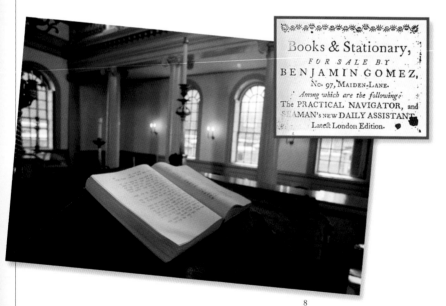

Books & Stationary,
FOR SALE BY
BENJAMIN GOMEZ,
No. 97, Maiden-Lane.
Among which are the following:
The PRACTICAL NAVIGATOR, and
SEAMAN's NEW DAILY ASSISTANT.
Lateſt London Edition.

FAR LEFT: *The Touro Synagogue, in Newport, Rhode Island, was built in 1773 to house one of the oldest congregations in the United States.*

LEFT: *Benjamin Gomez opened the first Jewish bookshop in the United States in 1791.*

RIGHT: *From the mid-1800s Jewish immigration stepped up. Single men set off on their own first, to establish themselves before bringing over their families.*

Arriving during a period of rapid geographic expansion, many German Jews along with Jews from Central and Eastern Europe joined the migration westward and established themselves in the developing western states. Following the route of the Erie Canal, communities were established in Chicago, Cincinnati, Indianapolis, and St. Paul. Wherever they settled, they formed a congregation and bought land for a cemetery.

The first Jews to emigrate were mostly young men. They joined up with scattered networks consisting of relatives and neighbors from the same European communities. Later, after the failed German revolution (1848), the profile of the immigrants changed. They were somewhat older than the first, more affluent, and better educated. These Jews often became peddlers or merchants, endeavors that called for small outlays of capital. Many went on to build substantial businesses and became part of the growing American middle class.

Many German-Jewish immigrants were part of the Reform Movement (*see page 77*) and the religious life of American Jews was colored by that connection. Founded in Hamburg, Reform Judaism aimed at winning civic equality and social acceptance in the modern world, and in order to do so, it did not enforce religious practices, such as keeping kosher (*see page* 88) or wearing beards or headcoverings, that separated Jews from other citizens. These immigrants came to America in search of democracy and civil rights. This is reflected in their overall concern for Jewish communal conditions. Strength would be found in numbers—religious, philanthropic, and fraternal organizations were founded during this period, such as the Hebrew Benevolent Society, Montefiore Mutual Benefit Society, the North American Relief Society for indigent Jews in Palestine, and many more. The B'nai B'rith also had its roots in the German-Jewish immigration to America.

The third wave of Jewish immigrants into the United States was by far the largest. Jews fleeing restrictions or even extreme persecutions (pogroms) came from Eastern Europe and Russia in large numbers. The profile of these immigrants differed from that of their predecessors. The first were

RIGHT: *B'nai Jeshuren, founded in 1827, is the second oldest Jewish congregation in New York. It was also known as the Elm Street Synagogue.*

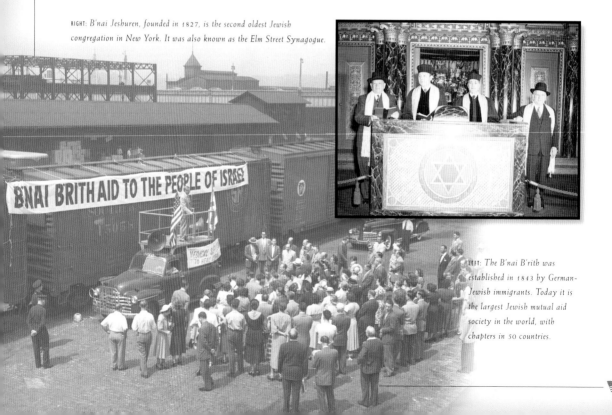

LEFT: *The B'nai B'rith was established in 1843 by German-Jewish immigrants. Today it is the largest Jewish mutual aid society in the world, with chapters in 50 countries.*

B'NAI BRITH AID TO THE PEOPLE OF ISRAEL

generally single men; the latter were entire family groups. Among the Russian and Eastern European Jewish masses who came to America were groups that maintained a strict, orthodox way of life.

These immigrants settled in the urban centers and went into handicraft trades in the garment industry or cigar-rolling factories until they raised the capital to go into business for themselves. They brought with them a rich Yiddish culture that expressed itself in journalism, fiction, poetry, and the theater.

As the Sephardim had once regarded the middle-class German Jews as upstarts, the German Jews now felt more "American" than the working-class Russian Jews. Class standing was not the only point of difference between the two groups. Accustomed to the insular life of the Pale (*see page 12*), the area between the Black and Baltic Seas where Jews were allowed to live, Russian Jews formed cohesive communities. They strongly upheld a sense of religion that permeated their lifestyle and offended their assimilated coreligionists. Their development and maintenance of a Yiddish culture (*Yiddishkeit*) also served to uphold their cultural differences.

RIGHT: *Reform Judaism, founded in Germany, was brought to America by immigrants in the mid-1800s. Today, it is stronger in the United States than anywhere else in the world.*

Between the two World Wars, Jews continued to join their families in the United States, and after the tragic events of World War II, thousands of homeless European Jews also entered the United States. Since then, American-Jewish communities have been enriched by the diversity of Jewish immigration, particularly from Iran and Syria. Indeed, the Sephardic communities of America are growing again. There has also been another influx of Russian Jews. Unlike the earlier Russian immigrants, these Soviet Jews have not had opportunity to maintain Jewish rituals and customs, or to study Hebrew, but they are finding thriving Jewish communities across the country.

LIFE IN EASTERN EUROPE

In 1791, Catherine the Great, czarina of Russia, created a zone of residence—some called it a zone of containment—for the Jews. This territory comprised more than 38,000 square miles (more than 1 million square kilometers), west of Russia stretching between the Baltic and Black Seas. The Jews called it "the Pale," and most were restricted to this area until after the Russian Revolution of 1917.

BELOW: *Hasidic Jews pray on the banks of the Vistula in Cracow, Poland, in this nineteenth-century painting,* Trumpets Feast, *by Alexander Gierymski.*

This region, east of Berlin and west of Moscow, was disputed territory for many years and included lands that today are known as Latvia, Lithuania, Poland, Belorussia, and Ukraine. But names of countries hardly mattered to the Jews. One could be born in Czarist Russia, then live in German territory, become a Polish citizen, then become Lithuanian, move back to German control, and

Baltic Sea

LATVIA

LITHUANIA

RUSSIA

RUSSIA

BELARUS

POLAND

THE PALE

UKRAINE

MOLDOVA

Black Sea

IRVING HOWE

"Bound together by firm spiritual ties, by a common language, and by a sense of destiny that often meant a sharing of martyrdom, the Jews of Eastern Europe were a kind of nation yet without recognized nationhood."

finally become a citizen of a Soviet Republic—and never leave the house where you were born. It was home to nearly all the world's Jews—in 1880, around 4 million Jews lived in the Pale, out of a world population of 7.7 million (another 2 million Jews lived outside the Pale but in Eastern Europe). They lived in nameless *shtetls* (small villages), as well as larger towns and cities such as Lodz, Warsaw, Minsk, Bialystok, and Vilna. They shared a rich culture and religion, and a language—Yiddish.

For several hundred years, Jewish culture flourished in Eastern Europe in the shtetls, or small towns, home to communities of devoutly religious Jews. In the shtetls, Jews were not enclosed by physical walls; instead, they were set apart by Jewish folk customs, religious observance, and a close-knit community and family life. In these insular, rural communities, the Jews of eastern Europe lived in a world where the pursuit of Jewish scholarship shaped their existence. Many men devoted their lives to study; most young boys studied at least until the age of 13, and even girls had some religious instruction, often in the home, from their mothers. Religious observances created the rhythm of life, from Sabbath to Sabbath, holiday to holiday.

LIFE IN THE SHTETL

While the synagogue was the spiritual center of the shtetl, the marketplace was the physical and communal heart of the village. Because Jews were restricted from land ownership, most earned their livings by crafts or trading. Market days were held once or twice a week, when peasants came from the surrounding lands to sell their produce and to buy material goods created by Jewish artisans or obtained by Jewish traders. Those men who did not devote their days to scholarship worked as cobblers, tailors, carpenters, glaziers, and draymen. However, wives and mothers often became the breadwinners for the family, producing goods at home that they could sell in the market, so that their husbands and sons could devote themselves to a life of biblical study.

No matter how poor a family was, some coins were set aside to buy either meat or fish for Friday evening and Sabbath dinner, served after the evening prayers at the synagogue. Part of the observance of the Sabbath was also giving to the poor, either money or food—*tzedakah*, or charity, was (and is) a central feature of Jewish life. There was a saying that a person could starve any day of the week, but nobody ever starved on the Sabbath. Since travel on the Sabbath was forbidden, if a stranger arrived in town on Friday night, he went to the synagogue knowing that someone would offer him hospitality.

ABOVE: *This synagogue in Prague was located underground, in a cellar, for safety.*

BELOW: *A Jewish water carrier struggles to earn a living in Vilna in 1920. Life in the shtetl was hard, but conditions were no easier in the big cities.*

Families were large, with three generations often living under one roof. Marriages were arranged by parents, often with the help of professional matchmakers. Although women were not given a voice in community affairs and they sat apart from the men in the synagogue, they were respected and honored in the family circle. They were responsible for keeping a Jewish home and for the household economy.

Shtetls were also united by mutual dependence. Each shtetl had a community council, often headed by the rabbi, that coordinated its various social welfare organizations. This way, the tradition of *tzedakah* was formalized and organized because each Jewish community ensured that it looked after its members.

By the end of the nineteenth century, the poverty in the Jewish settlements of the Pale was intense. Fathers and sons continued to attend to their scholarship, which did not bring any income to their families or their villages. There were countless legal restrictions on Jewish occupational rights. The few Jews who had worked as economic middlemen, dealing between peasant laborers and the nobility, found themselves squeezed out of the picture. Jewish traders had nothing to trade.

It was only inevitable that young people would start to flee the shtetls, making their way to the slums of Warsaw, Vilna, Lodz, Minsk, Bialystok, and other cities in search of a better life. These cities became centers of Jewish culture. Vilna, in particular, was known as the "Metropolis of Israel"

BELOW: *Although boys' education was a priority, girls also received schooling, often from their mothers. These girls are studying with a woman teacher in Laskirow, Poland, around 1910.*

ABOVE: *Jewish businessmen, like those depicted in*
A Hurried Speculation (1841) by Jan Felix
Piwarski, fell on hard times toward the end
of the nineteenth century.

ABOVE: *Some Jews left the Pale for a new life in Palestine, like these Russian men farming in a Jewish agricultural colony there in 1920. It had taken them 10 years to raise the money to emigrate.*

RIGHT: *In the ghetto of Vilna, Russia, businesses like this paper store (1922), served the Jewish community.*

FAR RIGHT: *Wagons travel to market near Piaski, Poland— many Jews in the Pale made ends meet by trading goods.*

and was renowned for its scholars. Odessa was to become prominent in the Zionist movement (*see page 80*). In the mid- to late-1800s, some Jews made their fortunes, and a Jewish middle class also emerged, benefiting from increasing industrialization and new avenues of trade. But for the most part, urban Jews continued to earn their livings as artisans, practicing traditional trades. Many urban Jews formed unions, consisting of people working in the same trades, to provide the mutual support that life in the shtetl had formerly offered.

For most Jews and non-Jews alike, living and working conditions in these cities were harsh. In response to conditions throughout the Pale, many Jews became politicized. One of the strongest new groups was the Jewish Labor Bund, created in 1897, which sought to transform the lives of Jewish working poor through socialist organizing and secular Yiddish culture. All through the 1880s and 1890s the Bund organized strikes among the workers of the Pale. Although these strikes did not achieve better working conditions, they were successful in planting the seeds of dissent. The theories of socialism, Zionism, and American freedom began to take hold in "Yiddishland." Many people began to think about emigrating—to Russia, or Palestine, or America.

The traits that characterized the Jews of the Pale of Settlement—a willingness to work hard and subsist on little, loyalty to family ties, respect for learning, rigid piety, and a moral obligation toward life—they brought with them to the New World.

THE GREAT WAVE
OF IMMIGRANTS

By the outbreak of the American Civil War, German Jews were already settled in 150 towns and cities around the country, although the East Coast held the greatest attraction. And by 1880, America's Jewish population had grown to more than 210,000, 80,000 of them living in New York. Some, like Isidor Strauss, set themselves up as merchants; Levi Strauss emigrated from Bavaria to New York in 1848 and then made his fortune selling clothes to miners in California. Businessmen such as Julius Rosenwald, who purchased Sears, Roebuck, and Company, imported the notion of a mail-order enterprise from Germany. There was even a flourishing soda-water industry to satisfy the new immigrants, who generally did not drink

RIGHT: *The business started by German Jewish immigrant Levi Strauss in 1848 grew into a huge multinational manufacturer and retailer by the end of the twentieth century.*

BELOW: *A German-Jewish immigrant, Julius Rosenwald, launched the famous Sears mail-order catalog.*

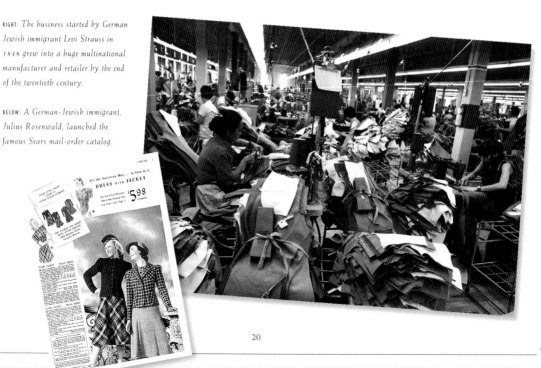

LEFT: *The Nobel Prize-winning physicist, Albert Einstein (second from left) became a U.S. citizen in 1935.*

LEFT: *Maurice Wertheim, New York banker, was elected President of the American Jewish committee in 1941, which was established in 1906 to protect the civil and religious rights of Jews.*

alcohol. Others became successful in banking—although Jews were rarely hired by American banks in those days. Jewish banking houses, such as those of the Guggenheims, Wertheims, and Baches, received financial resources from Jewish bankers in Europe.

Of course, not all German-Jewish businessmen made spectacular successes, but more of the first generation entered into business or other middle-class occupations than any other nineteenth-century immigrant group. Even with this material success, however, many German Jews, particularly among the elite, never lost their German identity. As one Chicago rabbi said: "I am a Jew, for I have been born among the Jewish nation. Politically I am an American, as patriotic... an American citizen as it is possible to be. But spiritually I am a German, for my inner life has been profoundly influenced by Schiller, Goethe, Kant, and other intellectual giants of Germany." Others considered their American residency a temporary step, until conditions in Germany calmed.

THE RUSSIAN EXODUS

The last two decades of the nineteenth century would see another type of Jewish immigrant to the shores of America, one who would not mind losing any previous national identity. Following the assassination of Czar Alexander II by radicals (one of whom was Jewish) in 1881, a wave of pogroms, or anti-Jewish riots, broke out in southern Russia. On April 27, 1881, the city of Yelisavetgrad was the site of the first pogrom; Kiev was the second, on May 8, 1881. During the last nine months of 1881, more than 160 towns and villages suffered cases of riot, rape, murder, and wanton destruction against their Jewish communities.

LEFT: *The assassination of Czar Alexander II of Russia was the catalyst for a wave of pogroms.*

BELOW: *The Jewish community of Kiev suffered a pogrom on May 8, 1881.*

RIGHT: *Jews crowd St. Petersburg's Baltic railroad station, after they are expelled from the city and forced to move to the Pale of Settlement.*

The May Laws of 1882, signed by Alexander III, restricted the rights of Jews to settle in the cities, curtailed their religious rights, and forced them to resettle in unfamiliar territory, restricting them to the Pale of Settlement (*see page 12*), which covered much of Eastern Europe. Under the terms of the new laws, Jews were prohibited from buying property, and their educational opportunities were limited. In addition, many Jews feared forced conscription into the Russian army because they believed that they would be required to convert and join the Russian Orthodox Church.

Even the forced movement of Russian Jews from Moscow, St. Petersburg, and countless small villages to the Pale did not stop the government campaign against them. Mary Antin remembered this period well: "The Jews who lived illegally without the Pale turned their possessions into cash and slept in their clothes, ready for immediate flight. Those who lived in the comparative security of the Pale trembled for their brothers and sisters without, and opened wide their doors to afford the fugitives refuge. And hundreds of fugitives, preceded by a wail of distress, flocked into

ABOVE: *The victims of a pogrom in Russia in 1905*
await identification. Continuing violence forced
many Jews to emigrate.

the open district, bringing their trouble where trouble was never absent, mingling their tears with the tears that never dried."

The resettlement program cruelly accomplished its purpose. The cities and towns in the Pale soon became overcrowded and it was almost impossible to earn a living. One complaint heard was: "There…are scores of watchmakers in small towns where the townsfolk have no watches." But sympathy for the plight of Jews was definitely not part of Czarist policy. The Russian Minister of Interior, Count Ignaitev, reminded a delegation of Jews, "The western borders are open to you." It was advice well taken. As Mary Antin remembered of Passover that year, "What said some of us at the end of the long service? Not 'May we be next year in Jerusalem,' but 'Next year in America!' So there was our promised land."

Between 1881 and 1914, close to 2 million Jews traveled to America, almost all of them Eastern European. Approximately one-third of all Eastern European Jews left their homeland, so that by 1903 Eastern European Jews constituted nearly 98% of all Jews coming to America.

ABOVE: *The Jewish cemetery in Vilna was all that remained of a once vibrant community that once called the city home.*

This was a Jewish migration only comparable to that following the Spanish Inquisition.

Unlike their German predecessors, when Russian and Eastern European Jews arrived in America, they did not look back. One Jewish immigrant, Dr. George Price wrote, "Sympathy for Russia? How ironical it sounds!...Am I not despised? Am I not urged to leave? It is impossible that a Jew should regret leaving Russia."

It is true that not everyone wanted to migrate. The most skeptical tended to be the most religious. Orthodox Jews thought living in America would weaken the faith, believing that America was a corrupt and sinful place where the Sabbath was not kept holy. Rumor had it that Jews in America did not even fast on Yom Kippur. Even the meat in America was considered *trayf* (unkosher). There were the few Jews who were prosperous enough that they had a stake in remaining in Europe. There were others who had received letters from America describing life in none too flattering terms. And there are always people who fear anything new and will do anything to avoid it.

But the more people left, the more people wanted to leave. Letters from former townsfolk who had already made the journey, raving about new possibilities, were circulated, read and reread. Whole families emigrated together. Skilled and unskilled workers followed the flow. Entire villages were swept up in this great migration. Agents from the steamship companies distributed propaganda, even in the smallest villages, painting visions of America as a land of riches and happiness.

It was said that there would be no return from the transatlantic journey. While in many ways this is true for all immigrants, it was doubly true for the Jews from the Pale—less than 5% of Eastern European immigrants returned to the old country. Like it or not, they were leaving their motherland for good. Jewish immigrants would change America, and in return America would change them.

The differences between the first wave of Jewish immigrants (German) and the last (Eastern European and Russian) were great. The groups differed in education, finances, culture, language, world outlook, ability to assimilate, and even the ways in which they practiced the same religion. German Jews did not exactly welcome their eastern brethren with open arms. Although they aspired to assimilation, they were still cast as outsiders and felt unsure of their place in the country. An inundation by "uncouth Asiatics" as the *Milwaukee Zeitgeist*, a Jewish publication, described them, would do nothing to alleviate this sense of insecurity. In Cincinnati, Isaac

M. Wise wrote: "We are Americans and they are not. We are Israelites of the nineteenth century in a free country, and they gnaw the bones of the past centuries....The good reputation of Judaism must naturally suffer materially, which must without fail lower our social status."

Over time, however, all Jews did learn to work together, even if it would take generations to do that on an equal basis. By the time the last European immigrants stepped ashore, German and Eastern European Jews had begun to realize that the two groups had more in common than previously thought. They would find out that in becoming American they had become one group— all Jewish Americans.

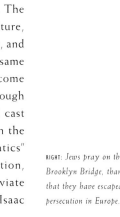

RIGHT: *Jews pray on the Brooklyn Bridge, thankful that they have escaped persecution in Europe.*

BELOW: *A crowd of Jewish refugees, awaiting permission to emigrate from Russia around 1910, present their documents for official approval.*

LEAVING HOME

Leaving home for the New World was an expensive and complicated proposition. Families had to sell everything to raise the money for the tickets. In 1890, a steerage ticket cost $15, but the fare went up to $34 by 1910. Many villages had ticket agents employed by the steamship companies, who would even sell tickets on an installment plan. Sometimes, fathers, along with the older sons and daughters, would make the voyage first, in order to find jobs and homes and earn the money to be able to afford to send for the rest of the family. But being able to purchase the ticket was only the beginning of a long and arduous journey into the unknown.

To get to America, one had to get to a port. In many cases, this was the most risky part of the long journey, because it was the least secure part of the trip. No one really knew what to expect on the overland journey to a port. There were no guidebooks for immigrants. Nearly all information was word of mouth. Many would-be emigrants, accustomed to sheltered lives in their shtetls, were

JACOB GLATSTEIN

(1896–1971), Yiddish-American writer/poet writing about his native Lublin, Poland, which he left in 1914

"Goodnight vast world
Giant world, stinking world…
And even though all has
been devastated
I am searching for the
dust in your dust
Desolated Jewish life"

BELOW: *Many Jews lived in abject poverty in the Pale of Settlement, and raising the money to emigrate was extremely difficult.*

HOLLAND

RUSSIA

GERMANY

UKRAINE

HUNGARY

ROMANIA

TRAVEL ROUTES

There were four main routes taken by Jews from Russia, Poland, Romania, and Austro-Hungary:

Jews coming from the Ukraine and southern Russia would cross the Austro-Hungarian border illegally, travel by train to Vienna or Berlin, and then make their way to one of the major ports of embarkation: Hamburg and Bremen in Germany; Rotterdam and Amsterdam in Holland; and Antwerp in Belgium.

Jews emigrating from western or northwestern Russia would sneak across the German border and then proceed to northern ports.

Jews from the Austro-Hungarian Empire would enter Germany legally and then proceed to Berlin and onward to any of the ports.

Jews from Romania traveled mostly through Vienna or Frankfurt and then up to Holland.

forced to deal with strangers for the first time in
their lives. Immigration was becoming a big business in Europe, and everyone stood to benefit.
Money was to be made from the immigrants—by
both Jews and gentiles. Abraham Cahan describes
entering Austria in 1882: "In the evening we
followed two young Ukrainian peasants to a small,
freshly plastered hut ....We waited a long time in
the hut before we realized we were being held for
more money. Having paid we moved on....We stum-
bled on endlessly. It seemed as if the border were
miles away. Then the peasant straightened up and
announced we were already well inside Austria."

The routes to the ports were never direct,
owing to the everchanging situations at borders or
roads. Most Jews in those years did not have proper
travel documents. Although this did not stop
them from emigrating, it did mean that it was more
difficult to travel. Jews were forced to cross
Germany in sealed trains because they were not
welcome there, but at the same time, Jewish
emigration was an economic boon for the country.
Albert Ballin's Hamburg-America Line alone was
making an annual profit of 10 million marks on the
emigrant trade, most of whom were Eastern
European Jews. The emigrants were always at the
mercy of the authorities, particularly at border
crossings. They were easy prey for hustlers of all
kinds offering them "quality" lodgings at special
prices or upgraded or fake tickets for trains or
steamer accommodations.

RIGHT: *Steamship lines made enormous profits from the torrent of Jewish emigration between 1880 and 1920. The Hamburg America Line alone made around DM 10 million a year just from the emigrant trade.*

Arrival at these ports did not mean the end of the migrants' problems. Port cities were especially dangerous because there were a whole array of vocations that existed to fleece the emigrant. There were hostel keepers, railroad employees, ships' officers and crews, and especially ticket agents. Many of these dealers were Jews who spoke Yiddish and exploited their victims' trust in them. Would-be emigrants also had to contend with the bureaucracy of the shipping lines. In Hamburg, for example, Jews were put through questioning, disinfecting, and quarantining before they were allowed to board their ships, and these inspections became stricter over time because steamship lines were required to return excluded immigrants back to Europe at their expense. As one emigrant described in a Special Consular report in 1904:

"Two weeks within high brick walls, several hundred of us herded in half a dozen compartments…sleeping in rows…with roll calls morning and night…with never a sign of the free world beyond our barren windows…. The greatest event was the arrival of some ship to take some of the waiting passengers. When the gates were opened and the lucky ones said goodbye, those left behind felt hopeless of ever seeing the gates open for them. It was both pleasant and painful, for the strangers grew to be fast friends in a day, and really rejoiced in each other's fortune; but the regretful envy could not be helped either.".

LEFT: *Before embarking, emigrants register their departure in the Registration Station in Leipzig, Germany, in 1908.*

TOP RIGHT: *People who could not read and write employed scribes, like Reb Moshe Yakov of Lukow, Poland, to compile the documents required to obtain permission to emigrate.*

As the situation in Russia worsened, the influx of Jews pouring into Western Europe reached a crisis point, and Western European Jewish organizations stepped in to help the refugees. The French Alliance Israelite Universelle, and other groups like it, which had been formed a few decades before to help victims of cholera epidemics, now sent committees to border towns to help the refugees with money, clothing, and medical care. These organizations worked to make the mass exodus as smooth as possible—this also meant that the immigrants would spend as little time as possible on Western European soil on their way to America.

THE CROSSING

BELOW: *People left Eastern Europe with their few remaining possessions, having been forced to sell off much of what they owned just to raise the fare.*

EDWARD STEINER, CLERGYMAN, 1906

Crowds everywhere, ill-smelling bunks, uninviting washrooms—this is steerage. The food, which is miserable, is dealt out of huge kettles into the dinner pails provided by the steamship company....On many ships even drinking water is grudgingly given.

When at long last the Jews made it to the ships, most were just grateful to have made it across Europe in one piece. They certainly were not prepared for a transatlantic journey of epic proportions. It is safe to assume that for the overwhelming majority this would be their first voyage on a ship; for many, it would probably also be the last, because they would be unwilling to undertake the journey more than once.

Living conditions in steerage (which cost $15 in 1890, but by 1910 had gone up to around $34, a small fortune for an impoverished emigrant) tended to be dormitory-like, with separate compartments for male and female passengers. The bunks were sacks of straw, each provided with a quilt for sleeping and a dipper for water. Toilet facilities were inadequate and showers were only introduced in later years. While kosher food was made available, it was not necessarily edible, so passengers often relied on the dried provisions they brought with them.

Accounts of the journey can speak for themselves. Here are some excerpts:

RIGHT: *Conditions for steerage passengers were arduous. It was often a great relief to escape from the cramped quarters to breathe fresh air up on deck.*

"We were huddled together in the steerage literally like cattle—my mother, my sister and I sleeping in the middle tier, people being above us and below us.... We could not eat the food of the boat since it was not kosher. We only asked for hot water into which my mother put a little brandy and sugar to give it a taste. Toward the end of the (14 days) trip when our bread was beginning to give out, we applied to the ship's steward for bread."

(Morris Raphael Cohen, from *A Dreamer's Journey*, about his crossing in 1892)

35

For many it was the first time they had ever left home, which made the experience all the more trying. Here is a woman writing in Yiddish more than 50 years after her arrival in 1891:

"The sky was blue—the stars shining. But in my heart it was dark when I went up on the ship.... We rode three weeks on a freight train so I had plenty of time to think things over. My future...where am I going? To whom? What will I do?...And then a real storm broke out. The ship heaved and turned. People threw up, dishes fell, women screamed...but in my heart I didn't care what happened."

Another immigrant from this period, described only as self-educated, reports: "On board the ship we became utterly dejected. We were all herded together in a dark, filthy compartment in the steerage....Wooden bunks had been put up there in two tiers....Seasickness broke out among us. Hundreds of people had vomiting fits, throwing up even their mother's milk....As all were crossing the ocean for the first time; they thought their end had come. The confusion of cries became unbearable."

But anticipation, a belief that new possibilities were going to open up and that dreams of a better future would become reality in the New World, sustained people throughout the difficult journey across the Atlantic. Eventually, the skyline of New York would finally appear on the horizon, signaling that the crossing was coming to an end, and that a new life was going to begin.

RIGHT: *The journey to America was often treacherous. Conditions onboard ship were cramped and unhygienic.*

LEFT: *Arrival in the United States: the moment that many Jewish emigrants had dreamed of during the hardship of the journey across the Atlantic.*

ARRIVING IN AMERICA

After what must have seemed to be an endless journey, arriving in New York harbor was an emotional experience. The view of the Manhattan skyline and the Statue of Liberty, the two great symbols of America, overwhelmed the steerage passengers, symbolizing all of what they had come to America for—freedom, opportunity, and hope. But the immigrants found very little of what the Statue of Liberty represented at Ellis Island.

New York was not the only port of entry. In 1903, Baltimore, Boston, Montreal, St. Johns, and Philadelphia were all flooded with immigrants. Jews were also making their way to the southwest via Galveston, Texas—more than 10,000 Jews came through Galveston in the first 15 years of the twentieth century.

But Ellis Island was by far the biggest port. It opened up as an immigration processing center in 1892, when the responsibility for immigration processing transferred from the states to the federal government (previously immigrants to New York passed through a center called Castle Island). There, the experience was dehumanizing and somewhat brutal, as immigration authorities had to clear up to 5,000 new entrants each day.

After being numbered and tagged, immigrants were split up, men in one line and women and

ABOVE: *A Russian Jewish girl waits for immigration clearance on Ellis Island. Her expression speaks for itself.*

RIGHT: *While their visas and other documents were inspected, tired immigrants waited in Ellis Island's main detention room.*

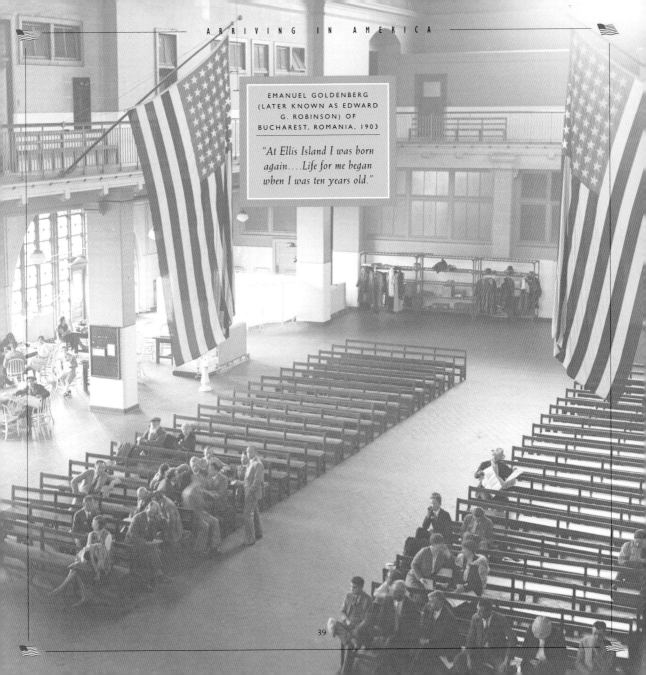

EMANUEL GOLDENBERG
(LATER KNOWN AS EDWARD
G. ROBINSON) OF
BUCHAREST, ROMANIA, 1903

*"At Ellis Island I was born
again....Life for me began
when I was ten years old."*

children in another. Then they were put into groups of 30 for an initial medical examination and processing. Manny Steen, who came through Ellis Island when he was 19, remembered this vividly. "Frankly, the worst memory I have of Ellis Island was the physical because the doctors were seated at a long table with a basin full of potassium chloride and you had to stand in front of them…and you had to reveal yourself…and the women had to open their blouses…this was terrible." Only around 10% of immigrants, of all nationalities, failed the health inspection. Those who needed healthcare were hospitalized and offered full treatment.

Following the medical examination was an immigration inspection. It was here that an immigration officer had the discretion to let would-be immigrants enter the United States—or to exclude them. There were several grounds for exclusion, in addition to disease. Inspectors were also trying to identify people with psychological problems, anyone with a criminal background, or anyone "liable to become a public charge," who would either try to make a living from crime, or be unable to support themselves at all. Also treated with suspicion were potential radicals or anarchists. If a newcomer failed to satisfy an inspector, he or she was sent to separate offices on the second floor for more in-depth examinations. Few were kept overnight, and only a very small minority did not make it to the mainland. Even after 1903, when all steerage passengers had to show about $30 in savings, the rate of exclusion for Jews at port of entry was negligible.

For a bewildered newcomer, exhausted from the steerage journey, the sense of powerlessness was intimidating. Strange people, dressed in strange uniforms and speaking in strange tongues, controlled their lives. Often immigrants found that their names were changed—legally— by immigration authorities who were unable

LEFT: *Immigrants' eyes are examined in 1920, part of a thorough health inspection. If a serious medical condition was discovered, prompt treatment was provided.*

RIGHT: *Immigrants who were detained were treated humanely. The meals they were offered were a vast improvement on the food available throughout the Atlantic crossing.*

to understand and Americanized what they thought they heard: Sasha became Charles, Roisl became Rachel or Rose. Julia Greenberg recalls her experience as a six-year-old girl: "My mother had what we call a featherbed, that she made of feathers plucked from ducks.... In order to make sure that we didn't bring in contraband, they searched your luggage....They came with a knife and cut it and the feathers were flying all over the place and my mother's tears were awful because this was her most prized possession."

But at the same time, the authorities tried to provide some succor to people who were exhausted, physically and mentally, from their journey. "They had long tables and they gave us some kind of meat and we looked at my mother whether we can eat it because it might not be kosher and my mother smiled and said 'eat it' because we didn't have a good piece of meat all the way through and we were just starving," remembers Estelle Bedford, who came to America when she was only five years old. "They called our name....We were

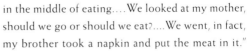

LEFT: *Having passed the rigid examination for entry in 1925, an immigrant family looks with hope at the New York City skyline while waiting for the government ferry to take them across to the city.*

BELOW: *Jews detained at Ellis Island build a succah in preparation for the holiday of Sukkot.*

in the middle of eating....We looked at my mother, should we go or should we eat?....We went, in fact, my brother took a napkin and put the meat in it."

Romanian immigrant Max Schnapp also described his reception at Ellis Island, in 1923, a little more kindly: "It was packed with people, packed with people. And there was a table where a commissioner sat there. He was a very nice man....Anyone he talked to he tried to relax them. He made a joke with them. He was very easy going."

The Hebrew Immigrant Aid Society (HIAS) and other charitable organizations had agents at Ellis Island to help out with interpreters and other advice, serving not only people who were detained but also new arrivals who were frightened and disoriented. The HIAS, for example, established temporary shelters and helped people track down their relations if they had failed to meet the boat; the American Jewish Women's Committee (Ellis Island) helped people find jobs; the United Hebrew Societies provided material assistance to detainees and contacted their relatives for them.

Even though this first encounter with a new bureaucracy was frightening, for most immigrants conditions on Ellis Island really did not matter. They were in sight of a new promised land, America, and they were met by their fellow Jews. The Czar, pogroms, and the poverty of Europe were behind them. Better times could only be waiting for them in this land of opportunity.

LOWER EAST SIDE AND
OTHER NEIGHBORHOODS

ANZIA YEZIERSKA, 1925

"What my mother and father and their mother and father never had a chance to give out in Russia, I would give out in America. The hidden sap of centuries would find release."

ABOVE: *Immigrants who have passed through the entry station on Ellis Island wait for the ferry that will transport them to New York City, where they can begin their new lives.*

BELOW: *The barge station at Ellis Island, shown here as it was in 1902, was known as the Castle. From here, immigrants set foot in New York City for the first time.*

Once their travel documents were stamped, the newcomers boarded a barge that took them to the southern tip of Manhattan Island. They were now in America. Five out of every six Russian and Eastern European Jews settled in urban communities, joining their compatriots. And the majority made Manhattan's Lower East Side their new home.

Between 1885 and 1899, 417,010 Jews disembarked in New York, and most of them remained there. By 1911, Jews constituted more than one-quarter of Manhattan's residents, and more than 500,000 Jews lived on the Lower East Side. More people crowded into fewer square feet of living space there than any other neighborhood in the United States.

In response to crowded conditions in New York City, the Industrial Removal Office (IRO) was formed in New York in 1901. Until its demise some 22 years later, it assisted more than 75,000 Jewish "Greenhorns" to move out of New York City and into 1,500 smaller communities around the country, including Champaign, Illinois; La Crosse, Wisconsin; Gary, Indiana; Galveston, Texas; and Cedar Rapids, Iowa, to name just a few. Newcomers were also sent to bigger cities, like Chicago, Cleveland, and Detroit, which already boasted large Jewish populations. By the end of the World War I, Chicago had a Jewish population of 200,000.

New York welcomed the Eastern European Jewish immigrants. In a speech in 1882, the mayor of New York City, William R. Grace, said:

"The citizens of New York have heard with sadness and indignation of the sufferings inflicted upon the Jews of Russia.... In this age, the recognized equality of all men, irrespective of their religious confessions, an essential element in American constitutions, is a principle and a practice which secures the loyal devotion of all classes. This is eminently true of the Hebrews, who constitute faithful citizens and subjects wherever accorded the rights of manhood.... We sympathize with our fellow citizens of the Hebrew faith in their sorrow for their afflicted brethren in Russia and in their energetic efforts for the welcome of the exiles."

At that time, living conditions on the Lower East Side were extremely difficult. The immigrants, often with large, extended families, occupied small apartments in the rows of dilapidated tenement buildings that lined the unpaved streets of the Lower East Side. The buildings, most constructed after the 1850s, were designed to accommodate many people. Their Italianate facades were copies of more expensive houses uptown, but their interiors were cramped and dark.

The apartments generally consisted of three rooms—one larger, front room and two smaller bedrooms. But despite these designations, all the rooms were used as bedrooms, because so many family members all lived together in these

RIGHT: *Life was not always easier here in the New World. Here, a family contemplates its future after being evicted from their apartment on the Lower East Side around 1910.*

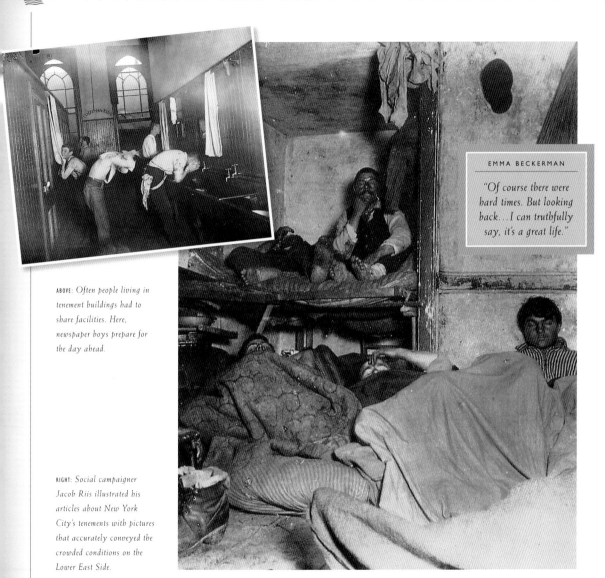

EMMA BECKERMAN

"Of course there were hard times. But looking back...I can truthfully say, it's a great life."

ABOVE: *Often people living in tenement buildings had to share facilities. Here, newspaper boys prepare for the day ahead.*

RIGHT: *Social campaigner Jacob Riis illustrated his articles about New York City's tenements with pictures that accurately conveyed the crowded conditions on the Lower East Side.*

factories and shops, especially in the clothing trade (*see page 58*). Others turned to peddling as a way to earn a living. By 1900 there were more than 25,000 pushcart peddlers and market stalls on the streets selling everything from shoelaces and shirt collars to fresh meat and vegetables. Some products were reassuringly familiar from the old country; others, such as bananas or processed foods, were new and exotic. Pushcarts offered a decent living, with wages comparable or better than those of the sweatshops, and they also provided more flexibility and allowed men the time to continue with their studies at the same time as they could support their family; also,

their wives and children were able to help out. Some peddlers even managed to save enough to invest in setting up in small stores.

The peddlers' pushcarts set the tone for the humming street life of the Lower East Side. In the shtetls, the market square had always been the center of community life, particularly for women. In the city, similarly, everybody lived life out on the street, enjoying some fresh air (there were no parks nearby), visiting peddlers and local stores, sitting on the front stoop, sharing gossip, and creating a community into which newcomers felt immediately welcomed, and which guaranteed mutual support.

RIGHT: *Hester Street, lined with Jewish-owned stores and businesses, was at the heart of the Lower East Side*

ABOVE: *Because tenement apartments were so cramped,
people escaped to the streets to watch the world go by, sitting
on the stoop or browsing stores and market stalls.*

LANDSMANSCHAFTEN

As strangers in a strange new world, it was only natural for immigrants to turn to each other, and to Landsmanschaften, mutual benefit societies composed of people who had come from the same communities in the Old World, were soon organized. These societies offered immigrants a place where they could get news from home, raise money in emergencies, locate family members, and receive inexpensive medical and legal services and help in burying the dead. Landsmanschaften also served as informal housing and employment agencies, and they organized lectures and social events—even dances—that strict families felt comfortable allowing their daughters to attend.

In 1905 there were more than 1,000 Landsmanschaften in New York, the majority located in lower Manhattan; by 1910, there were 2,000. As late as 1938 there were still some 500,000 members of Landsmanschaften in New York alone, with another 250,000 members in the rest of the country. About 85% of members were foreign-born—their Americanized children rarely relied on this form of support.

LEFT: *Jews gather on the streets of the Lower East Side to celebrate Rosh Hashana, around 1910.*

There were also many other self-help organizations set up by Jews for Jews, following a long tradition of charitable giving. "It is more than 240 years since the Jews were first admitted, by special license as it were, to the New Netherlands, on the express condition that 'the poor among them should not become a burden to the company or to the community, but be supported by their own nation,' and most loyally have they kept the compact that long ceased to have force to bind. Their poor are not, and never were, a burden upon the community," wrote social campaigner Jacob Riis in 1896. "The Jewish charities are supported with a generosity and managed with a success which Christians have good cause to envy."

Often associated with synagogues, Jewish welfare organizations, like the United Hebrew Charities, were established as early as the 1700s, and prosperous German Jews were dutiful in donating to them. However, these organizations struggled to keep up with the demands placed on them by the heavy flow of new immigrants—and many German Jews resented the new immigrants—so Russian Jews soon enough set up their own. The instant a new arrival set foot in the United States, he was met and assisted by a range of charities offering advice, healthcare, free temporary housing, and help finding jobs and settling in. Other groups, such as the Educational Alliance or the Baron de Hirsch Fund, provided education and training, teaching English and other skills to both adults and children.

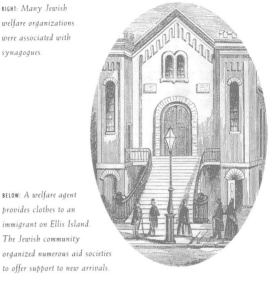

RIGHT: *Many Jewish welfare organizations were associated with synagogues.*

BELOW: *A welfare agent provides clothes to an immigrant on Ellis Island. The Jewish community organized numerous aid societies to offer support to new arrivals.*

YIDDISH CULTURE

The immigrants brought with them a vibrant culture. The medium for this culture was their language—Yiddish. Much to the chagrin of their assimilated German coreligionists, Yiddish became the language of the street, the home, the store, the factory, and the synagogue.

To satisfy the community's hunger for information and knowledge, Yiddish newspapers, magazines, and books were published. The Yiddish press began with weekly papers filled with discussions of religious issues and stories from "back home." By the 1890s, dailies began to come off the presses. By far the most popular daily was the *Jewish Daily Forward*, a mainstream paper that was launched in 1897 by Abraham Cahan, a Jewish socialist and journalist. Hundreds of Yiddish publications were started in the first two decades of the twentieth century, including Yiddish dailies in Chicago, Philadelphia, Cleveland, and Montreal. In addition to news and information, they also published work by Yiddish writers such as Isaac Bashevis Singer (*see page 99*). And the dailies were not all. There were also innumerable magazines appealing to both men and

ABOVE AND LEFT: *The Yiddish language has thrived since the arrival of Jewish immigrants in the United States. Throughout the Jewish-American community, signs in both Yiddish and English can be seen on store fronts, synagogues, in the workplace, and so on.*

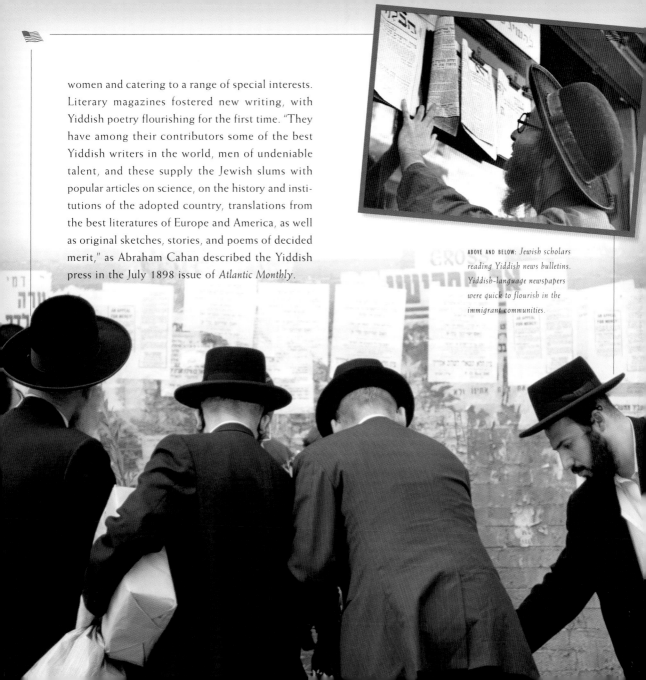

women and catering to a range of special interests. Literary magazines fostered new writing, with Yiddish poetry flourishing for the first time. "They have among their contributors some of the best Yiddish writers in the world, men of undeniable talent, and these supply the Jewish slums with popular articles on science, on the history and institutions of the adopted country, translations from the best literatures of Europe and America, as well as original sketches, stories, and poems of decided merit," as Abraham Cahan described the Yiddish press in the July 1898 issue of *Atlantic Monthly*.

ABOVE AND BELOW: *Jewish scholars reading Yiddish news bulletins. Yiddish-language newspapers were quick to flourish in the immigrant communities.*

Starting in the 1880s, New York's great Yiddish theater began to portray and satirize the lives, hopes, and ambitions of the immigrants. There was a great repertoire of material, ranging from translations and adaptations of classics to plays written in Yiddish by Yiddish playwrights. While escapist, light entertainment was popular, dramas treating subjects close to home, like the conflict between parents and their Americanized offspring, were also very well attended. Adaptations of Shakespeare, some altered to suit religious mores, were also big draws. By 1918 there were 20 Yiddish theaters in New York, located on or near Second Avenue, the "Jewish Broadway." There were some 200 traveling companies, and a number of permanent Yiddish theaters in larger cities around the country. Some of the biggest names in American film and theater, including Stella Adler, Paul Muni (born Muni Weisenfreund), and Molly Picon, got their starts in the Yiddish theater.

"Slowly, as immigration diminished, the ethnic theaters petered out, but the Yiddish theater

RIGHT: *During the 1920s and 1930s, the Yiddish Art Theater was just one of many similar theaters to portray Jewish-American immigrant life.*

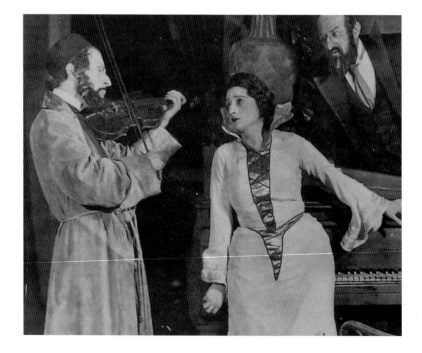

LEFT: *Stella Adler, star of Yiddish film and theater, with playwright Clifford Odets (right) and her brother Luther Adler.*

outlasted them all, in spite of the fact that the younger, American-born generation no longer could speak, or even understand, *mamaloshen*, the mother tongue (so called, I suppose, because mama did all the talking)," explained Molly Picon. "Since Mama was so anxious to see her children become Americans, not remain greenhorns, she urged them on to learn English, to be able to go to college, to become a Somebody. Unfortunately, she didn't realize then what a wonderful heritage and what a vivid, juicy language they were losing and would never be able to recapture."

ABOVE RIGHT: *Molly Picon, the popular Jewish stage star as she set sail on the S.S. Rex for a vacation in Palestine in 1933.*

RIGHT: *Paul Muni accepts an Oscar for his starring role in* The Story of Louis Pasteur *in 1936. Muni's career began in New York City's Yiddish theater.*

THE GARMENT INDUSTRY

For many of the East European Jews, the garment industry, with its long hours, low pay, and its sweatshops (the name comes from the idea of "earning bread by the sweat of their brows"), offered the first opportunity for employment. By the time that the Eastern European immigrants arrived, New York City was the center of the American garment industry, producing three-quarters of all women's clothes, as well as a large proportion of men's clothing. The majority of the factories were owned by German-Jews and were located on the Lower East Side , where new

waves of immigrants provided a ceaseless source of cheap labor. Conditions in the factories were terrible. Young girls (around 70% of factory workers were women, and the majority were under the age of 20) and men worked in crowded conditions, usually in a loft room that was cold in winter and stifling in summer. Weekly wages for a 16-hour day, six days a week, were $6–$10 for men and

FAR LEFT: *In this sweatshop on Ludlow Street in 1890, boys toiled alongside men for only pennies a day in hot, cramped conditions.*

BELOW: *Recent immigrants worked up to 16 hours a day, six days a week, in order to earn enough money to live.*

$4–$5 for girls and women. Many had to pay the foreman an initial sum of money simply to get a job and then undergo days or even weeks of unpaid training. They were charged for the needles they used and the power supplied to the factory, at a 20% profit for the owners. Workers were also taxed for the chairs on which they sat, made to pay for clothes lockers, and fined for coming to work five minutes late. Those who complained about conditions were fired.

If the factories were bad, the sweatshops were even worse. They were usually located in tenement buildings, often in the apartment of the owner, who had subcontracted work from a factory. In many cases there were no windows or other ventilation in the room. The wages were lower and the hours longer, and adults and children alike worked six days a week for 50 cents to $1.50 a week. Other families took in homework, sewing or rolling cigars in their already overcrowded apartments— even children as young as three years old were expected to help out.

Many workers felt that they had nothing to lose by organizing unions. "So far from depressing wages and bringing down the standard of living, the Jewish working man has been among the foremost in the struggle for the interests of the wage-earning class of the country," wrote Abraham Cahan in *Atlantic Monthly* (1898). Jewish union activists would bring a new radicalism and vitality to the American labor movement.

In 1886, the American Federation of Labor was formed, with Samuel Gompers, a Jewish immigrant and former cigar maker, as president. In an attempt to oppose the sweatshop system, Jewish immigrants helped to form two large labor unions, the International Ladies Garment Workers Union (ILGWU) in 1900 and the Amalgamated Clothing Workers of America in 1914. The United Hebrew Trades, in reality a federation of Jewish unions, had been established as early as 1888. In 1909, with the support of the United Hebrew Trades, a series of strikes erupted in New York. These strikes were unprecedented for their size, duration, and fury.

The first strike was by the bakers: 2,000 went on strike in the spring. They were joined in November of that year by 20,000, mostly female, shirtwaist makers. One of the local shops the shirtwaist makers struck against was the Triangle Shirtwaist Company.

At 4:35 p.m. on March 25, 1911, a fire broke out in the Triangle Shirtwaist Company and spread quickly among scraps of cloth littering the floor. In the 18 minutes it took to bring the fire under control, 146 workers, most of them young Jewish and Italian girls, burned or jumped to their deaths. The charred bodies spoke of unimaginable pain. The East Side broke into scenes of hysteria, demonstrations, and mass meetings. The front page of the *Jewish Daily Forward* printed this eulogy: (opposite)

As a result of the tragedy, the owners of the Triangle Shirtwaist Company were placed on trial for manslaughter. However, it could not be proven that they knew a stairwell would be locked on the day of the fire, so they were not prosecuted. Three months after the fire, the New York legislature created the Factory Investigating Commission whose job was to check factories for fire hazards, unsafe machines, and poor health conditions.

Over whom shall we weep first?
Over the burned ones?
Over those beyond recognition?
Over those who have been crippled?
Or driven senseless?
Or smashed?
I weep for them all.

LEFT: *Many mothers took in partwork so they could look after their children while they sewed. Here a woman delivers completed garments to the factory.*

RIGHT: *Family members arrive at the New York City morgue to identify the victims of the Triangle Shirtwaist Company fire that killed 146 workers, mainly young women.*

JEWISH GANGSTERS

MEYER LANSKY, AS AN OLD MAN,
TALKING ABOUT THE POGROMS IN HIS
NATIVE GRODNO, POLAND

"Most people have never heard of Jewish gangsters. They do not believe they ever existed. The very idea of a Jewish gangster goes against basic stereotypes of Jews, stereotypes that explain the place of Jews in the world. Jews are physically unthreatening office creatures."

"One man—I don't remember his name…held a meeting at my grandfather's house. 'Jews,' he shouted, 'why do you stand around like stupid sheep and let them come and kill you, steal your money, kill your sons, rape your daughters.…Aren't you ashamed?…You must stand up and fight. A Jew can fight.'…This speech is burned in my memory."

ABOVE LEFT: *Meyer Lansky (left) arrives at court in 1978, accompanied by his lawyer, to face a grand jury investigation in Florida.*

LEFT: *Arnold Rothstein's coffin is carried to the hearse for his Orthodox funeral. He was murdered by an unknown gunman.*

Crime was nothing new in urban America when the Eastern European Jews arrived. Harsh economic conditions drove some Jews to the underworld, and some were very successful in that life.

One of the "pioneers" of Jewish crime was Arnold Rothstein, who became one of the great gambling kingpins of his day, and he was also believed to have been a major player in the narcotics trade. He was later to be immortalized in F. Scott Fitzgerald's *The Great Gatsby* (1925) as Meyer Wolfsheim, the man who fixed the 1919 World Series. When Rothstein was murdered, in 1928, at the age of 46, he received an Orthodox Jewish funeral.

Prohibition ushered in opportunities for a new generation of criminals. People like Meyer Lansky, Dutch Schultz (born Arthur Flegenheimer), Louis "Lepke" Buchalter, and Benjamin "Bugsy" Siegel were notorious criminals involved in bootlegging, prostitution, and union busting, particularly in the garment industry. Lepke ran his gang, Murder Inc., out of Brownsville, Brooklyn. Bugsy Siegel launched a hotel, the Flamingo, in Las Vegas, which opened the doors for the mob in what was then a backwater town in the middle of nowhere. (Gambling havens were to be the post-Prohibition future for the mob.) "We're bigger than U.S. Steel," said Meyer Lansky, And he was right, in his time.

RIGHT: *During Prohibition, gangsters profited by selling outlawed liquor in speakeasies.*

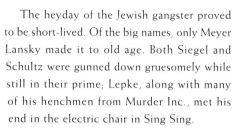

DETECTIVE DIVISION
CIRCULAR NO. 11
AUGUST 8, 1939

POLICE DEPARTMENT
CITY OF NEW YORK

CLASSIFICATION

$25,000 REWARD
DEAD OR ALIVE

TWENTY-FIVE THOUSAND DOLLARS will be paid by the City of New York for information leading to the capture of "LEPKE" BUCHALTER, aliases LOUIS BUCHALTER, LOUIS BUCKHOUSE, LOUIS KAWAR, LOUIS KAUVAR, LOUIS COHEN, LOUIS SAFFER, LOUIS BRODSKY.

WANTED FOR CONSPIRACY AND EXTORTION

The Person or Persons who give Information Leading to the Arrest of "LEPKE" will be fully protected, his or her identity will never be revealed. The information will be received in absolute confidence.

RIGHT HAND

LEFT HAND

DESCRIPTION — Age, 42 years; white; Jewish; height, 5 feet, 5½ inches; weight, 170 pounds; build, medium; black hair; brown eyes; complexion dark; married, one son Harold, age about 18 years.

PECULARITIES—Eyes, piercing and shifting; nose, large, somewhat blunt at nostrils; ears, prominent and close to head; mouth, large, slight dimple left side; right-handed; suffering from kidney ailment.

Frequents baseball games.

Is wealthy; has connections with all important mobs in the United States. Involved in racketeering in Unions and Fur Industry, uses Strong-arm methods. Influential.

This Department holds indictment warrant charging Conspiracy and Extortion, issued by the Supreme Court, Extraordinary Special and Trial Terms, New York County.

Kindly search your Prison Records as this man may be serving a Prison sentence for some minor offense.

If located, arrest and hold as a fugitive and advise the THE DETECTIVE DIVISION, POLICE DEPARTMENT, NEW YORK CITY, by wire.

Information may be communicated in Person or by Telephone or Telegraph, Collect to the undersigned, or may be forwarded direct to the DETECTIVE DIVISION, POLICE DEPARTMENT, NEW YORK CITY.

LEWIS J. VALENTINE, Police Commissioner

TELEPHONE: SPring 7-3100, SPring 7-2722, SPring 7-1366 or CAnal 6-2000

The heyday of the Jewish gangster proved to be short-lived. Of the big names, only Meyer Lansky made it to old age. Both Siegel and Schultz were gunned down gruesomely while still in their prime; Lepke, along with many of his henchmen from Murder Inc., met his end in the electric chair in Sing Sing.

The Jewish gangsters were the children of immigrants, either born in the United States or coming over with their parents when they were very young. They tried, as best they could, to conceal their activities from their family and neighbors and did not encourage their children to follow them into a life of crime. Before his execution, Louis "Lepke" Buchalter ensured a trust fund was set up for his sons' college education.

As Jews started becoming more affluent, so, too, did Jewish criminals decline in numbers. In 1921 Jews represented 14% of New York State's prison inmates; by 1940, the figure dropped to 7%. In 1910, Jewish women made up 20% of the female prison population in New York; by 1940 this was down to just 4%.

LEFT: *The New York City police department circulated this poster during their hunt for Louis "Lepke" Buchalter, who was wanted for conspiracy and extortion.*

LEFT: *Arthur Flegenheimer (left), better known as Dutch Schultz, leaves court during his trial on charges of income tax evasion in October, 1935.*

BELOW: *A week later, Dutch Schultz was gunned down by rival gangsters in a New Jersey restaurant.*

BECOMING AMERICANS

World War I ended the era of mass Jewish immigration to the United States, as wartime conditions, followed by restrictive quotas, stemmed the human tide. Soon, for the first time in many decades, the majority of American Jews would be native-born. The main focus of Jewish life ceased to be the problems of immigration and absorption. Instead, Jewish Americans entered a period of relative stability—the children of immigrants moved up into the middle class, and families moved to more affluent and fashionable neighborhoods, where they established new institutions, such as synagogue centers and progressive Hebrew Schools.

It became quite apparent that the Eastern European Jews could and would assimilate into American society. The question was not if they could become American but, if by becoming American, they could still be Jews.

> ### FRIEDA SCHIFF WARBURG
>
> *"To me, and to all our family, it has always been of the utmost importance to know one's past and to live up to it with pride and a true sense of responsibility."*

LEFT: *Two girls join the May 1 Labor Parade in New York City in 1901. Their banners, calling for an end to child labor, are written in English and in Yiddish.*

BELOW: *A schoolroom on the Lower East Side in the 1890s is crowded with eager young students.*

SETTLEMENT HOUSES

Beginning in the 1880s, well-established German Jews embarked on a systematic campaign to "Americanize" newly arrived Eastern European immigrants whose style, appearance, and behavior were so different from theirs—and so un-American. Their charitable work involved the efforts of teams of social reformers, settlement house workers, and home economists, who tried to encourage the newly arrived immigrants to leave behind them their "backward ways" and adopt instead the styles and mores of the American middle class. Novelist Anzia Yezierska described, with her tongue firmly in her cheek, how one "friendly visitor" or food missionary did her work: "By pictures and lectures she shows us how the poor people should live."

The charities already established by German-American Jews were unable to cope with the vast influx of Eastern European immigrants, and new

solutions had to be found. One was the settlement house system, which forever changed the way social workers operated. Settlement workers lived in the community to teach immigrants not only by means of formal classes and home visits but also by example. Rather than believing that poverty indicated a lack of morals, on the nineteenth-century model, these new social workers maintained that education and Americanization were the key to improved conditions.

LEFT: *These children are about to leave the Henry Street Settlement House to enjoy two weeks in the countryside, thanks to donations by wealthy New York City philanthropists.*

ABOVE: *Lillian Wald, the daughter of German-Jewish immigrants, was the founder of the Henry Street Settlement.*

BELOW: *A nurse from the Henry Street Settlement stops to talk with some Jewish children in 1910.*

The Henry Street Settlement is one example. It was founded by Lillian Wald, the daughter of German-Jewish immigrants. A trained nurse, she first visited the Lower East Side as part of her post-graduate training and was shocked by the conditions in which she found people living. With a colleague, she moved to the area, renting a house and concentrated her efforts on women and girls in the Jewish community. She tried to teach newly arrived immigrants about modern American notions of hygiene and nutrition, encouraging them to include more fresh fruits in their diet in place of pickles and more fresh than smoked or salted meat. In the settlement house, she set up a model apartment, in which she could demonstrate "healthful" styles of home decoration and cleaning methods. She also set up vocational training programs for young women and became an advocate of public health services. By 1916, funded by philanthropist Jacob Schiff, the Henry Street Settlement had more than 100 nurses on staff to serve the Lower East Side.

Often welfare workers making their rounds found to their surprise that these "greenhorns" had a rich and meaningful culture of their own. They were particularly impressed by the tight community and familial networks that they found among the Eastern European Jews. One social worker, Mary Kingsbury Simkhovitch, another daughter of German-Jewish immigrants and the founder of Greenwich House, observed, "a solid family life where each was dependent on the other. Clash and conflict were necessary corollaries of this closeness, but there was something loving about such a home life in which no individual could live for himself alone..."

When a family arrived from Europe, everyone, young and old, contributed to the financial stability of the family. The father would work more or less full time (often allowing time for religious observance or scholarship), the mother would take in homework, usually sewing, and even the children would help out, working in the home or in the sweatshops. Although child labor was illegal, it was very common—if an inspector arrived, children were simply hidden from their prying eyes, in closets, under piles of fabric, even in shipping boxes.

RIGHT: *A public health nurse from the Henry Street Settlement visits a mother and her children in a Lower East Side tenement. The nurses and social workers concentrated their educational efforts on women and children.*

and 50% at New York University. The same sea change was occurring at other colleges along the East Coast and in major cities across the country. While elite universities had tolerated the well-off and assimilated German-Jewish students who joined their rolls in the mid-nineteenth century, the children of Eastern European immigrants were a challenge to the status quo.

In order to limit the numbers of Jewish students, many private universities established quota systems, despite the fact that these violated federal antidiscrimination laws and outraged liberal thinkers. It was at this time that universities began including personal interviews in the admissions process, as a way to gauge an applicant's social standing. Others required psychological testing, which screened out "ethnic" applicants—through this kind of screening, Columbia University, in the heart of New York City, succeeded in reducing its intake of Jewish students by almost 50%.

Not even the Ivy League quota system could stop Jews from acquiring higher education. In 1916–17, of the 385,000 college students in the country 14,500 were Jews—about 3%. In 1937, of the 1,148,000 students, 105,000 were Jews—close to 10%. Their success in obtaining higher education was apparent as the number of highly trained Jewish professionals multiplied. In 1930, Jews made up 25% of New York's population but provided 65% of its lawyers, 64% of its dentists, and 55% of its physicians. In the 1930s, many Jews also started joining the faculties of colleges and universities, and once on the inside, they encouraged their administrations to backtrack on their quota systems. By the 1940s, Jews were also establishing their own institutions of higher learning, such as New York's Yeshiva University, first established in 1928 as Yeshiva College of Secular Studies, or Brandeis University in Massachusetts, the first Jewish-sponsored nonsectarian college.

LEFT: *A Yeshiva university student volunteers in a local public school. Its Stern College for Women was the only Jewish liberal arts college for women in the United States.*

ABOVE: *During the 1920s, Columbia University in Manhattan used "ethnic screening" to reduce the number of Jewish students offered admission.*

RIGHT: *Prayer at Yeshiva University, 1944. By this time Jewish Americans had begun to set up their own colleges of further education.*

LEFT: *The "radio priest," Father Charles Coughlin, was notorious for his antisemitic remarks during his broadcasts.*

ANTISEMITISM

Antisemitism peaked in America in the inter-war years. A variety of respectable institutions—schools, camps, country clubs, even places of employment—imposed restrictions against Jews. Public attacks on Jews through the media were commonplace, from figures like the Detroit radio priest Father Charles Coughlin, industrial magnate Henry Ford, or U.S. ambassador to London Joseph Kennedy. Real estate advertisements often included the coded phrase, "Near Catholic and Protestant churches" in an attempt to keep Jews from moving into certain neighborhoods.

Before 1941, as Arthur Hertzberg said, "Almost no Jew could make a free, personal decision about his education and career. At every turn, the fact of his Jewishness meant that many, if not most, options were simply not available to him." A 1936 survey in *Fortune* magazine found that very few Jews had achieved senior management positions in any industry other than entertainment. Those who did succeed often concealed their Jewishness, like Gerald Swope, president of General Electric between 1922 and 1940. From the 1950s, the situation eased, as Jews were more commonly found among the senior executives of Fortune 500 companies—and in the neighborhoods, schools, and clubs from which they had once been excluded.

COHESION

In response to antisemitism, Jewish communities pulled together, and the old barriers between German Jews and Eastern European Jews fell away. Leaving behind Old World divisions, they began to form a truly American-Jewish community.

Today there are many ways to live openly as a Jew in America. Reconstructionism, the newest form of Jewish observance to arise in the United States, maintains that Judaism is a cultural construct, and that it is possible to live a Jewish life without being religiously devout. On the other end of the spectrum, American Orthodox Judaism still holds complete commitment to Jewish law, although even within Orthodoxy, there are modernists, and it works alongside other Jewish denominations on issues of common interest.

In between these two poles, Conservative and Reform congregations continue to hold their place throughout the United States. Conservative Judaism grew rapidly in the United States; the Reform Movement, which was elaborated in the United States by German-Jewish immigrants bringing the ideas of the Enlightenment overseas, is stronger here than anywhere else.

Although there is concern that Judaism is becoming secularized, it remains true that more than 80% of Jewish children receive some form of religious training, and respect for its festivals and ceremonies, such as bar and bat mitzvah (*see page 94*), is strong among all denominations.

RIGHT: *Community leader Stephen S. Wise addresses a crowd of more than 250,000 Jews massed to protest against antisemitism at a 1933 rally in New York City.*

FAR LEFT: *Jews, as well as African Americans, were targeted at a pro-segregation rally in Montgomery, Alabama.*

Hasidim

Between 1947 and 1952, some 100,000 European Jewish survivors of World War II arrived in the United States under the Displaced Persons Act. Nearly half of these were of Hasidic background.

Hasidism was strongest in Poland: of the 3.5 million Jews living in Poland immediately before World War II, the vast majority of them were Hasidim of the "Aleksander" dynasty. (The Aleksander community today is now nearly extinct, because it was unable to rebuild itself after the war, unlike many other communities.) There are perhaps a dozen major Hasidic movements today, the largest of which (with around 100,000 followers) is the Lubavitch group, headquartered in Brooklyn, New York. Other groups include the Bobov, Bostoner, Belzer, Gerer, Satmar, Vizhnitz, Breslov, Puppa, Bianer, Munkacz, and Rimnitz. These communities are thriving, despite the fact that four out of five Hasids died in the concentration camps. Hasidic communities maintain a tight inner structure, a high morale, and an extremely strict religious outlook. They are the last bastion of the Yiddish language.

LEFT: *A young boy helps out in the family business in the Williamsburg section of Brooklyn, New York, the heart of the Satmar Hasidic community.*

ABOVE: *Hasidic men celebrate in their section of a bridal feast. In Orthodox synagogues, men and women worship and celebrate apart.*

ZIONISM

With the creation of the State of Israel in 1948, the Zionist dream had come true. After the trauma of the Holocaust, Jewish-American morale was boosted immeasurably. Support for the new state became one of the focal points of American-Jewish philanthropy, and it was a symbol around which many American Jews united.

There was little obvious support for Zionism before World War I. German-American Jews were concerned that Zionism would encourage separatism as well as accusations of disloyalty, and they maintained that, as Americans, their allegiance was to the United States. Eastern European immigrants, who had experienced such violent anti-Jewish feeling before coming to the United States, were in favor of a Jewish homeland, but they were primarily concerned with economic survival, and their political and social activism was directed toward the labor movement.

It was Louis Brandeis, ironically a child of German-Jewish immigrants, who gave Zionism a higher public profile. A progressive lawyer with a successful practice in Boston, Massachusetts, he became the first Jewish Supreme Court Justice in 1916. But before that, Brandeis became curious about Zionism when he discovered that one of his

ABOVE: *Jewish refugees flock to Israel after the end of World War II. Their banner says, "Keep the gates open, we are not the last."*

ABOVE: *Louis Brandeis, (front row, first left), the first Jew to be appointed to the U.S. Supreme Court, was an influential campaigner for the Zionist cause.*

relatives had been a Zionist activist; this interest was heightened by his advocacy work on behalf of disadvantaged Jewish immigrants. From 1915, he was committed to the cause and became its public spokesman in the United States. His linking of Zionism with American values won a great deal of support: "The highest Jewish ideals are essentially American in a very important particular. It is Democracy that Zionism represents. It is Social Justice which Zionism represents, and every bit of that is the American ideal of the twentieth century." Within two years, the American Zionist movement had increased its membership ten times over, and the issue was in the public eye.

LEFT: *Jewish settlers meet in the Palestinian desert in 1909 to cast lots for building sites, after deciding to found Tel Aviv as an all-Jewish city.*

"A DISNEYLAND WITH KNISHES"

Jews vacationed in Pennsylvania's Poconos, the Berkshires of Massachusetts, and even in some more accessible areas of the Adirondacks farther north in New York state—but the Catskills, in Sullivan County two hours north of New York City, were the undisputed capital of the Borscht Belt, as these resorts were collectively known.

Borscht, a red beet soup invented in Russia, was, and is, a favorite of Jewish families. When the

BELOW: *In 1905, this railroad station in the Catskills was only open in the summer, to bring vacationers to the resort hotels.*

ABOVE: *The Grand Hotel was one of the big hotels built in the region to cater for their guests' desire for luxury.*

BELOW: *Successful businessman and socialite Kingdon Gould and his family headed to the Catskills every summer.*

people of the Lower East Side began setting up summer colonies of their own, they carried their borscht kettles with them. Later borscht, served with potatoes and sour cream, was a regular fixture on the tables of all the hotels and boarding houses that catered to Jews.

From the late 1890s onward, city dwellers were drawn to the Catskills as a way to escape the unhealthiness of the ghetto. Tuberculosis and other diseases were rampant in the city, and relatives would send family members to boarding houses to try to recover—or to die. Initially, people tended to board at houses operated by their own countrymen; so Russian or Polish or

Hungarian-Jewish boarding houses sprang up. Other boarding houses catered for members of specific occupations, including garment workers or cigar makers or union members.

As New York Jews prospered, the idea of spending the summer in the mountains took hold. It was common for husbands to send families "away" for the summer while they stayed behind in the city to work, visiting the family on weekends. And as more people discovered the region, bigger hotels appeared to cater to more demanding vacationers. By the 1950s there were more than 500 hotels, bungalow colonies, and other settlements.

FOOD AND FESTIVITIES

Although today Jewish food often means "kosher style" rather than kosher, for a people who have spent most of their history moving from place to place, food represents stability and endurance. It not only brings people together—food also brings the past back home. The Jewish holidays serve a similar purpose. Celebrating together, Jewish families, and the broader Jewish community, maintain a meaningful link with the past at the same time as they are affirming life.

As Jewish Americans dispersed around the country, they never forgot the food of their childhood, or the food of their ancestors' childhood. Jewish New Yorkers, now living in the suburbs, will tell you that the best pickles come from the Lower East Side. Jews living in Miami will tell you they can't get a decent bagel, because you can only get good bagels in New York. Jews in Los Angeles will tell you the smoked fish on the West Coast is tasteless. It is nothing like the fish they had as children in Brooklyn or the Bronx. Today, some of New York's Jewish restaurants are famous throughout the country, even if they are no longer

LEFT: *A New York deli offers a wide variety of bagels. Once an exclusively Jewish food, they are now part of the culinary mainstream.*

in business, and Ratner's blintzes and Nathan's Coney Island frankfurters are decidedly part of the Jewish culinary heritage. Other names of repute include Yonah Schimmel Knishes Bakery, Guss's Pickles (now known as Essex Street Pickles), and of course, Bernstein-on-Essex (now closed), which offered kosher Chinese food, and Schapiro's House of Kosher and Sacramental Wines, a little sweet but interesting.

RIGHT: *Two men enjoy some Kosher Chinese food at Bernstein-on-Essex, on New York's Lower East Side.*

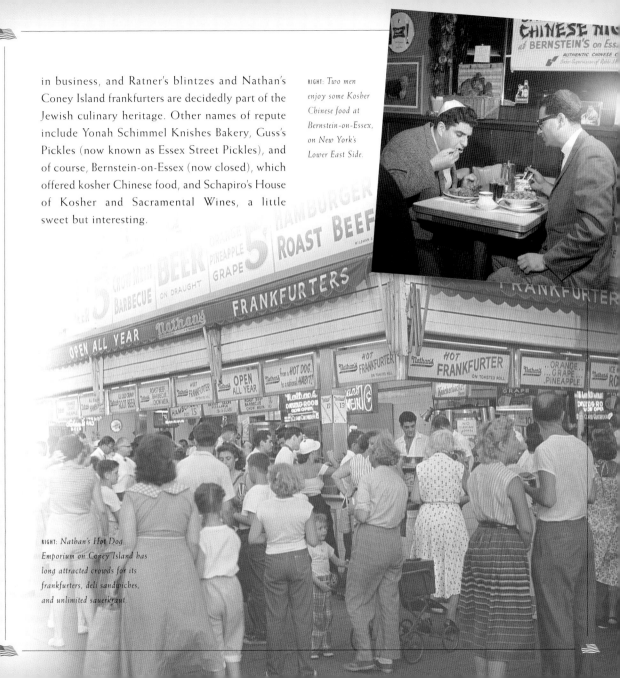

RIGHT: *Nathan's Hot Dog Emporium on Coney Island has long attracted crowds for its frankfurters, deli sandwiches, and unlimited sauerkraut.*

KEEPING KOSHER

While many German-Jewish immigrants followed the Reform tradition and did not follow the rules of Kashrut, most of the Russian and Eastern European Jewish immigrants who succeeded them were more observant, keeping kosher homes and observing all the holidays. Around the turn of the twentieth century, the community was so unified in its observance that some holidays were celebrated communally; for example, on the Lower East Side, there was a public burning of food that was not kosher for Passover. For these Jews, religious observance did not have to be hidden behind the doors of synagogues and private homes.

As the numbers of observant, Orthodox Jews multiplied, so a demand for kosher food and other traditional items grew. The production of matzo in New York City expanded rapidly between 1880 and 1920. Most matzo factories (bakeries) were located on the Lower East Side. So, too, were kosher wineries, where alcoholic beverages for the holidays were produced and sold. The slaughtering and meatpacking industry also expanded to accommodate a rising demand for kosher meat. The wholesale value of kosher food increased 70% between 1900 and 1909, and by 1916, kosher meat retailers in the city rang up more than $50 million in sales. By 1930 there were 7,500 kosher butcher shops in New York City; by 1934 there were about 12,000 kosher food processors and dealers.

Because demand for kosher food was so sudden and large, kosher certification remained problematic for decades, and efforts at regulating kosher food caused rifts in the community. These conflicts culminated in the "kosher meat riots." The first of these boycotts occurred in 1902 when the kosher butchers raised their prices dramatically because the packers had raised their prices. The Eastern European women of the Lower East Side, who had seen the good work of union activists in the garment industry, quickly organized a protest. A boycott of kosher butchers was accompanied by a demonstration during which meat was dragged outside the shop and ruined by being doused with gasoline and set alight. The boycott that followed the riot ultimately forced the butchers to close their shops in support until the packers backed down and lowered their prices. Similar incidents took place in 1910, 1929, and 1937 in New York and Chicago.

CHOICE GROCERIES FOR PASSOVER,
פסח
AT D. BEHRMAN'S NEW STORE,
172 BOWERY
Opposite Delaucy Street, NEW-YORK.
Which will be Superintended by L.M. RITTERBAND.

The subscriber begs to inform you, that he has made the necessary arrangements for the ensuing holydays, and will keep a full assortment of Groceries, also, every other article suitable for the occasion; and guarantees the same to be of the most superior quality, and at the lowest market prices, delivered free of expense to any part of the city. The goods will be ready for sale on the 3d of April, to which the subscriber respectfully solicits your custom.
D. BEHRMAN,
172 BOWERY, Opposite Delancy Street.
☞Orders received immediately if required.☜
הגדה של פסח In Hebrew and English For Sale.

Groceries für פסח.

Der Unterzeichnete eröffnet am 3ten April seine Niederlage von Groceries, von bester Qualität für die zukünftigen Feiertage פסח, unter der Aufsicht von L. M. Ritterbänd. Es wird alles zum billigsten Preise verkauft und kostenfrei zu irgend einem Theil der Stadt gesandt.
D. Behrman,
172 Bowery, gegenüber Delancy Street.
☞ Orders werden jetzt angenommen wen man es verlangt.
JACKSON, Cheap Printer, 190 Houston Street, and 205 Bowery.

FAR LEFT: *In 1848, a Lower East Side grocer advertises the range of Kosher-for-Passover goods available to his customers.*

BELOW: *A sign in a grocery store indicates which wines are Kosher for Passover.*

☆ THIS SECTION KOSHER FOR PASSOVER WINE

RIGHT: *In a poultry slaughterhouse, a shochet kills chickens according to the laws of Kashrut, ensuring that the animal feels no pain.*

LEFT: *A New York matzo factory prepares unleavened bread for the Passover celebrations in 1889.*

DELIS

Around the time of the American Civil War, a German-Jewish immigrant, Issac Gellis, moved his kosher sausage operation from Berlin, Germany, to Essex Street, on New York's Lower East Side. This was when the Jewish deli was born in America. His first customers were men on their own, who had no wives or mothers to cook for them, but soon even families in which the women worked became the loyal clientele of the hundreds of delis that opened in Jewish neighborhoods. Greenhorns happily consumed cured meats like salami, corned beef, tongue, and of course, pastrami. The latter is a unique, culinary creation of the American delis—a brined cut of beef coated with pepper and spices and then smoked (there is a Romanian meat called pastrami, but it is salted mutton that is cooked before it is eaten). While some delis were also restaurants, all offered quick service and most delis sold the meat in sandwiches—on rye bread. Other specialties included knishes, potato and flour dumplings that could be stuffed with a variety of fillings, like cheese or kasha, which are similarly portable. And both knishes and sandwiches were accompanied by pickles. Respecting the rules of Kashrut, those delis that served meat did not serve dairy products, but other delis specialized in dairy, selling smoked and salted fish instead of meat.

By the mid-1930s New York boasted some 5,000 delis—such as Katz's, the Stage Delicatessen, and the Second Avenue Delicatessen, to name just a few—some more famous than others, some more kosher than others. Jewish delicatessens quickly spread throughout the country, first with German Jews and then with Eastern European ones, all the way to California.

TOP: Katz's Deli was immortalized in the movie, When Harry Met Sally.

LEFT: Customers swarm Isaac Gellis' kosher butcher on Essex Street, after it reopened following a meat shortage in 1946. Cured meats, like salami, and hot dogs were brought to America by Jewish immigrants.

RIGHT: Katz's Delicatessen on Houston Street, in New York's Lower East Side, still serves up fantastic, overstuffed deli sandwiches to its many hungry patrons.

"We get a good deal of Jewish delicatessens in Hollywood," Orson Welles once wrote, "Without pastrami sandwiches there could be no picture-making." The most venerable of the dairy restaurants is New York City's Ratner's, "In good taste since 1905." Advertised as "the East Side's premier dining place," in the 1940s Ratner's served 2,500 customers a day, dispensing 100 portions of gefilte fish on weekdays—twice that much on weekends—along with countless portions of blintzes and pirogen.

As the garment industry moved uptown, delis and dairy restaurants moved with the factories, becoming part of the character of the new garment district. At restaurants like S&H Dairy Kosher Vegetarian Restaurant or the Vitamine Vegetarian and Dairy Restaurant, customers could lunch on "the best and most nutritious foods that money could buy." But not all Jewish restaurants were delis; others aimed to be more upmarket, such as Felix's Kosher Dining Room, which was touted as the "Jewish Delmonico's." The advertising for Garfein's Kosher Family Restaurant, an East Side Waldorf Astoria, claimed, "Among the happiest moments of your life you will recollect those spent in Garfein's Kosher Family Restaurant."

Bakeries and appetizer stores also became integral parts of Jewish culinary life. The bakeries make rye bread, pumpernickel, bagels, and bialys. On holidays like Purim they bake triangular, filled pastries called hamentaschen, to celebrate a victory over the Persians many centuries ago. Braided

challah bread is baked for the Sabbath. The appetizer stores specialize in delicacies like smoked fish, herring, pickles, and olives.

Jewish specialties are not only eaten by Jews. Today, bagels and lox or overstuffed deli sandwiches or frankfurters or pickles—all brought to the United States by Jewish immigrants, are part of the American eating experience.

And although a great many of the old kosher restaurants have gone out of business because their clientele has moved out to the suburbs, Jewish cooking continues to evolve. Delis will always be popular, but they are only the public face of Jewish cuisine. Home cooks continue to devise new ways to prepare old favorites, inspired by numerous specialist cookbooks appealing to every taste and diet.

FAR LEFT: *The deli counter is never quiet at Zabar's, one of New York City's most prestigious delicatessens.*

LEFT: *Located on the Upper West Side, Zabar's sells a range of goods that appeals to New York tastes and to the most sophisticated palates.*

RIGHT: *A customer studies the food at a kosher meat market in Brooklyn, New York.*

RIGHT: *Students gather round their Rabbi during a Purim celebration in a yeshiva in Philadelphia. One student wears a mock beard on the one day that masquerading is traditionally permitted.*

CELEBRATIONS

Food usually plays an important part when Jews gather to celebrate holidays or other special occasions. Even if Jewish Americans don't keep kosher during the year, they still prepare traditional foods for the holidays: Passover has its ritual seder meal; Rosh Hashanah has honey cakes, Yom Kippur has a special meal to break the fast, Purim has hamentashen, and the list goes on.

The celebrations of bar or bat mitzvah, which mark a young person's coming of age, include banquets that bring families and friends together with food, drink, and music. After weddings, bar and bat Mitzvah celebrations are the biggest catered kosher affairs American Jews participate in.

While the bar mitzvah, dating from the fourteenth century, is a tradition taken from the Old World and given a life of its own in the New World, the bat mitzvah, a similar ceremony for girls, was created in America. The first bat mitzvah was not celebrated until1922, when Judith Kaplan (the daughter of Rabbi Mordechai Kaplan, the founder of Reconstructionism, *see page 77*), was the first to be so honored. Since then, Conservative Jews and Reform Jews have also begun to celebrate bat mitzvahs. Confirmations, celebrated in Reform and Conservative congregations to mark the end of a young person's formal religious education at age 15 or 16, are also an American innovation. They developed first in Reform congregations, which believed that 13 was too young an age to take on the religious responsibilities of an adult.

Chanukah is a holiday held in great affection by young and old alike. But the shape it takes today bears no resemblance to the way it was celebrated in the Old World. Actually quite a minor holiday on the religious calendar, it is not celebrated with a special service in the synagogue, as is Passover, for example. Chanukah only became as festive as it is today after the Eastern European immigrants arrived in the United States. For the new immigrants, Christmas represented a challenge. Since the 1890s, gift-giving had been associated with the holiday, and it was marked by major retail promotions. At first, immigrants felt that one way to assimilate was by joining the consumer flow and buying presents. As the *Forward* wrote in December 1904, "The purchase of Christmas gifts is one of the first things that proves one is no longer a greenhorn." Buying presents did not make a person any less Jewish, it just allowed them to participate in the secular side of the festivities.

From the 1920s, Jewish storekeepers started to promote Chanukah gifts and special merchandise, soon wooing Jews away from Christmas and allowing them to transfer their retail fervor to their own holiday. In Eastern Europe, there had been a tradition of giving "gelt" (Chanukah money) to children on the fifth night of Chanukah, and gift-giving could be seen as an extension of that practice. Today, in addition to traditional practices, such as lighting a menorah, playing with a dreidl, and eating latkes, Jews celebrate Chanukah with parties, decorations, and presents—and chocolate "gelt" always figures prominently, a link between the old and the new.

LEFT: *A girl becomes a bat mitzvah at a synagogue in Minneapolis. The ceremony for girls, parallel to the boy's bar mitzvah, is an American innovation.*

Some painters, like Max Weber (1881–1961), took an almost poetic look at Jewish-American life. The son of Russian Jews, he came to America with his family when he was ten years old. His family was poor but he managed to study art at the Pratt Institute in Brooklyn before going to Paris.

Although his early work is Cubist, later in his career he became more representational, and he used his Jewish background in works such as *The Hasidic Dance* and *Adoration of the Moon*.

Other painters had more of a social agenda. Ben Shahn (1898–1969) once said to his wife, "It's all right to have a soft heart, so long as you have a hard eye." The Lithuanian-born painter and photographer was a social critic his entire professional life. After coming to United States in 1904, he attended New York University, City College of New York, and the National Academy of Design. Eventually he studied abroad where he collaborated with Mexican muralist Diego Rivera on public mural projects. Shahn eventually returned to the United States to join the federally sponsored Farm Security Administration, for which he took photographs of people suffering from poverty. Shahn once summarized his stance on social injustice like this: "I hate injustice. I guess that's about the only thing I really do hate." Shahn's most famous painting is *The Passion of Sacco and Vanzetti*, which was assembled in France and unveiled at Syracuse University in 1967.

LEFT: *After moving to New York from Russia when he was ten years old, Max Weber painted many visions of Jewish life.*

RIGHT: *The work of Ben Shahn (seated right, on the desk) was energized by his commitment to fighting injustice.*

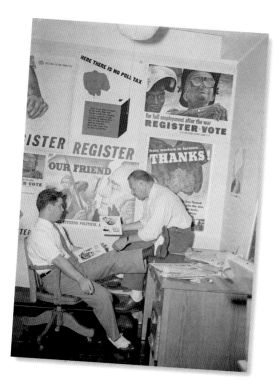

LITERATURE

If Jews are the people of the book, they are also people of books. Literature plays an important role in most Jewish households, and many Jewish writers have drawn on their backgrounds for their stories and novels.

The first Jewish writers in America wrote in Yiddish, their native language. On the Lower East Side, groups like the Sweatshop Poets and Di Yunge (the young ones) established a new tradition of Yiddish poetry. The Sweatshop poets were concerned with conditions of the workers—and in fact, like Morris Rosenfeld, considered to be the best exponent of the style, most of them were workers in the garment factories. On the other hand, Di Yunge were modernist poets who were not politically engaged.

As the Eastern European Jews acculturated, most ceased to write in Yiddish. One notable exception is Issac Bashevis Singer (1904–1991), the Nobel Prize-winning writer who came to the United States from Poland in 1935. In fact, Singer never wrote in English, and all his works have been translated from Yiddish. Educated to be a rabbi, Singer drew heavily on his Polish background, creating stories about Polish-Jewish communities before the Holocaust. He was also heavily influenced by Jewish mysticism and explained the supernatural in his writings by saying, "I would say that I believe in free will and at the same time in

Shahn was able to benefit from the change in fortunes for artists after the 1940s. As Jewish Americans became more affluent, they also became more interested in visual arts. Many contemporary artists, including Shahn, Robert Motherwell, Louise Kaish, Adolph Gottlieb, Boris Aronson, and others, were invited to create works for new synagogues being built in communities across the country, and patrons, both Jewish and gentile, enabled them to create countless masterpieces.

destiny…all our passions and everything were not created just by us. They have been created by higher powers." Among his works are *The Magician of Lublin, A Crown of Feathers, Enemies,* and *Yentl the Yeshiva Boy*—later to be made into a film by Barbra Streisand. Jewish spirituality would continue to influence Jewish writers, such as Bernard Malamud (1914–1986) and Cynthia Ozick (1928–).

During the 1920s and 1930s, the Lower East Side was the inspiration and setting for some notable works by Jewish writers, all of whom were concerned with issues of assimilation and acculturation. These were the themes of Anzia Yezierska (*see page 68*), in her novels, such as *The Bread Givers* (1925), as well as for the fiction of Abraham

TOP: *Isaac Bashevis Singer, shown here in Miami in 1981, wrote exclusively in Yiddish, despite living in America for much of his life.*

LEFT: *Barbra Streisand made Isaac Bashevis Singer's* Yentl the Yeshiva Boy *into a successful Hollywood movie musical.*

RIGHT: *Many Jewish novelists and poets have written works that portray Jewish-American life in all its complexity.*

Cahan, the founder-editor of the *Forward*. Later in the 1930s, Michael Gold, with *Jews Without Money* (1930) and Henry Roth, in *Call It Sleep* (1934), would create indelible portrayals of the struggle to Americanize.

It was after World War II that a new tradition of Jewish-American fiction would arise, created by the children of immigrants. These writers, although educated and assimilated, were also totally Jewish and their cultural and religious backgrounds pervaded their work. Saul Bellow (1915–), who grew up in a Yiddish-speaking household, wrote novels that looked uncompromisingly at urban life. His later works in particular focus on Jewish intellectuals who are challenged by everyday realities.

Similarly, the poet, writer, and political activist Grace Paley (1922–) set her work in the city, crafting portraits of working-class New Yorkers.

Philip Roth (1933–), on the other hand, sets his work in the suburbs. He came to fame with *Goodbye, Columbus* (1959), an uncompromising look at Jewish middle-class values and lifestyles. Most of his later work features the character of Nathan Zuckerman, a Jewish novelist, and play with the line between autobiography and fiction.

Assimilated Jews are not the only subjects. *The Chosen* (1967) by Chaim Potok (1929–2002) was the first book to portray Orthodox Jews as central characters in a realistic work. Centering on the conflict between the religious and the secular in

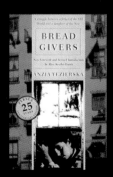

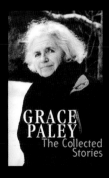

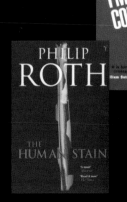

ABOVE: *Playwright Arthur Miller (center) with Jo Mielziner (left), building designer, and Elia Kazan, co-director of Lincoln Theater.*

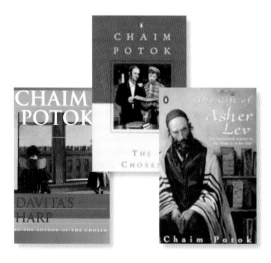

Jewish life, it is a powerful coming-of-age novel that has remained widely read. Pearl Abraham, with *The Romance Reader* (1996) and *Giving Up America* (1998) has continued the tradition of writing about Orthodox Jews, offering a rare glimpse of the Hasidic community.

One of America's most famous playwrights, Arthur Miller was born in New York in 1915. He was profoundly influenced by the ruin of his family's fortunes during the Depression. His plays, like *Death of a Salesman*, are all socially oriented, in the Jewish tradition, although they do not necessarily focus on the Jewish-American experience. *The Crucible* (1953), ostensibly a story about the Salem Witch Trials of the seventeenth century, is also an allegory about the Communist witch hunts of the 1950s—Miller himself was hauled in front of the House Un-American Activities Committee in 1956, and asked to give evidence about people he might have met at a meeting of the Communist Party ten years earlier. When asked to give a reason for the success of his plays, Miller once replied, "In one way or another, different kinds of people, different classes of people apparently feel they're in the play. Why that is I don't really know."

LEFT: *Chaim Potok featured Orthodox Jewish characters in his work, such as his popular coming-of-age novel,* The Chosen.

RIGHT: *Arthur Miller is one of the most respected and prolific American playwrights. His plays, such as* The Crucible, *shown here in performance, display his commitment to tackling important social issues.*

Arthur Miller **The Crucible**

Arthur Miller
A View from the Bridge/All My Sons

MUSIC

Jewish-American composers have continued in a rich tradition of both liturgical and popular music. Their music has often been distinguished by their willingness to incorporate a variety of styles and cultures. They have used elements from both black and white traditions, European and existing American styles, to create specifically American music.

Just as Eastern European immigrants began to flow into the United States, the American popular musical scene was exploding. Vaudeville shows and theatrical revues touring the country were fuelling a demand for sheet music. The music industry responded, and music publishers hired

ABOVE: *Tin Pan Alley fostered the songwriting talents of many famous composers, including Jerome Kern (far left), Oscar Hammerstein (seated at the piano), and Irving Berlin (far right).*

LEFT: *Russian-born Irving Berlin, seen here at the piano, was the composer of the popular anthem, "God Bless America."*

staff composers and lyricists to satisfy this new market. Many music publishers were based in New York City on West 28th Street between Broadway and Sixth Avenue—Tin Pan Alley. This was where many of the best Jewish composers got their start.

Born Israel Baline in Russia, Irving Berlin (1888–1988) came to New York with his family when he was five. His father was a cantor, and he grew up in a musical home. By the time he was 14, he was working as a singing waiter in Chinatown, where he wrote his first song *Marie from Sunny Italy*. In 1909 he began working as a staff lyricist on Tin Pan Alley. Berlin's influence on popular music was vast. Like many of his contemporaries, he was influenced by the American popular music of the time, which came out of the African-American minstrel and vaudeville tradition. Jewish performers were also making their name in vaudeville, performing the kind of music Berlin was writing: singers Al Jolson and Sophie Tucker both donned blackface to perform in vaudeville. Berlin's ragtime compositions, such as his first hit, "Alexander's Ragtime Band," so encapsulated the sound that he was once accused of "having a little colored boy in his closet" to write his music. In addition to the scores for many stage and film musicals, he is renowned as the composer of some quintessentially American music, including *Easter Parade* and *God Bless America*—not bad for a man who could not read or write music.

BELOW: *The daughter of Russian immigrants, Sophie Tucker, center, got her start in vaudeville. Her shows were enlivened by her risqué sense of humor and the occasional remark in Yiddish.*

RIGHT: *Born Asa Yoelson in Lithuania in the late 1800s, Al Jolson ran away from home in his teens to break into entertainment. He starred in the first "talking picture,"* The Jazz Singer.

Brooklyn-born George Gershwin (1898–1937) also came out of Tin Pan Alley, though he had a classical musical training behind him. Where Berlin was influenced by ragtime, Gershwin was inspired by jazz and blues, also African-American musical forms. While some of his compositions are unabashedly populist, like "Lady, Be Good," or "Funny Face," he also wrote more complex pieces combining elements of jazz and classical music, such as "Rhapsody in Blue." His brother, Ira (1896–1983) wrote the lyrics for many of his songs.

Aaron Copland (1900–1990) represents a different side to Jewish-American musical achievement: although he did not write "popular" music per se, he did want to create very American music that would appeal to a wide audience. The son of Russian-Jewish immigrants, he was first taught to play the piano by his sister, and by the time he was 15, he was determined to become a composer. He composed music both in the United States and in Europe before making his name in his 20s with some complex and quite "European" compositions. From around 1935, he tried to make his music more accessible, rather than composing "in a vacuum," as he said at the time. He also was determined to create specifically "American" music and found influences in jazz and blues and in American folk music, which he used in symphonic compositions as well as film scores (like *Our Town*, 1940) or ballets such as *Billy the Kid* (1938).

ABOVE: *The Gershwin brothers, George and Ira, were responsible for some of the greatest show tunes of all time.*

RIGHT AND BELOW: *The Gershwin brothers composed the songs in* Porgy and Bess, *but George also composed more complex instrumental pieces, such as "Rhapsody in Blue."*

IT'S GERSHWIN! IT'S GLORIOUS! IT'S GREAT!

SAMUEL GOLDWYN PRESENTS THE MOTION PICTURE PRODUCTION

PORGY and BESS

Hailed wherever it has opened! ONE OF THE YEAR'S 10 BEST!

SIDNEY POITIER · DOROTHY DANDRIDGE · SAMMY DAVIS, JR. · PEARL BAILEY

DIRECTED BY OTTO PREMINGER

COLUMBIA PICTURES

BELOW: *Aaron Copland's musical virtuosity is evident in the breadth of his compositions, ranging from complex symphonic pieces to show tunes.*

Ovation

Gershwin
Rhapsody in Blue
An American in Paris
Lullaby · Cuban Overture

Katia & Marielle Labèque
The Cleveland Orchestra
Riccardo Chailly

DECCA

TELARC

COPLAND
The Music of America

Fanfare for the Common Man
Commissioned by
The Cincinnati Symphony Orchestra in 1943
Rodeo
Appalachian Spring
Quiet City
Billy the Kid

Erich Kunzel
Cincinnati Pops Orchestra

successes of 20 to 30 new films each week. Once luxurious "picture palaces" opened to show longer films, demand rose even more. There, Jewish producers like Carl Laemmle at Universal Pictures, William Fox at Fox Film Corporation, the Warner Brothers, Harry Cohn at Columbia Pictures, Samuel Goldwyn, and Louis B. Mayer created the Hollywood of legend. Goldwyn's life story is typical of this breed of film entrepreneur: born Shmuel Gelbficz in Poland, he came to America when he was 12 years old. His first job was as a glove salesman, but he soon got into movies by buying a nickelodeon.

Fierce competitors, these men were united by their ambition and their desire to assimilate into the mainstream of American society. They cooperated when they had to: when they were barred by all the country clubs in Los Angeles, they

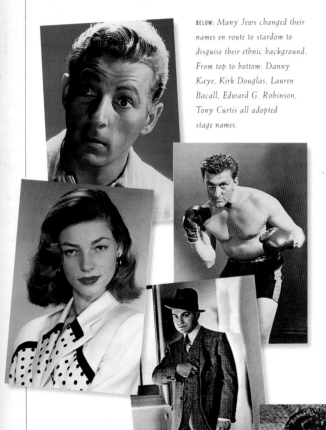

BELOW: Many Jews changed their names en route to stardom to disguise their ethnic background. From top to bottom: Danny Kaye, Kirk Douglas, Lauren Bacall, Edward G. Robinson, Tony Curtis all adopted stage names.

LEFT: Samuel Goldwyn, right, takes a break from production work on Guys and Dolls to visit his son, Samuel Goldwyn, Jr., left, on the set of The Deadly Pacemaker. They are joined by the film's star, Robert Mitchum.

founded their own. Their wish for social inclusion and their fervent belief in the American Dream also shaped the kinds of movies made in Hollywood. In its heyday in the 1930s and 1940s, the Hollywood studios made films that showed American life in the best possible light, where self-improvement and redemption were always possible.

But not just the producers were Jewish—so, too, were many of the stars of the silver screen, like Kirk Douglas (born Issure Danielovitch), Lauren Bacall (Betty Joan Perske), Tony Curtis (Bernard Schwartz), or Edward G. Robinson (Emmanuel Goldenberg). These actors changed their names to conceal their religious background, to avoid offending the audience for the studios' big-budget movies—which was around 90% Christian. Sometimes it was not only their names that were changed: David Kaminsky had to dye his hair blond as part of becoming Danny Kaye. Although audience demographics have altered, actors still change their names: Winona Ryder, for example, was born Winona Horovitz.

Despite the studios' Jewish ownership and management, they did not stand up to the House Un-American Activities Committee, which rampaged through the creative echelons of Hollywood in the late 1940s and early 1950s, searching out alleged Communists, most of whom were Jewish. Of the

LEFT: *Seven Hollywood writers and directors arrive at court to face charges of contempt of Congress after refusing to testify in front of the House Un-American Activities Committee.*

studio bosses, only Samuel Goldwyn refused to blacklist writers who had been questioned by the HUAC; some of the other studios were so cautious that they would not use writers who they thought might be questioned by the HUAC.

Nor did they make films featuring Jewish characters or storylines. *The Jazz Singer* (1927), the story of a Jewish son who wants to sing jazz rather than follow in his father's footsteps and become a cantor, was a rare, early example. It was not until the late 1960s, with *Funny Girl* (1968), the story of entertainer Fanny Brice and starring Barbra Streisand, and *Goodbye Columbus* (1969), based on the Philip

ABOVE: *Barbra Streisand starred in* Funny Girl (1968), *the story of the Jewish entertainer, Fanny Brice.*

RIGHT: *Woody Allen, the Brooklyn-born comedian and filmmaker, has mined his Jewishness to great comic effect in his films and writing.*

BELOW: *Producer and director Steven Spielberg was personally committed to the making of* Schindler's List *(1993), about the Holocaust.*

WOODY ALLEN
DIANE KEATON
TONY ROBERTS
CAROL KANE
PAUL SIMON
JANET MARGOLIN
SHELLEY DUVALL
CHRISTOPHER WALKEN
COLLEEN DEWHURST

"ANNIE HALL"
A nervous romance.

Roth story of the same name (*see page 101*) that Jewish heroes and Jewish issues began to be seen frequently on screen.

Today, Jewish stories are commonplace in the movies, and filmmakers, like Brooklyn-born Woody Allen or Steven Spielberg have no need to deny their Jewish roots. At the same time, the profile of Hollywood is changing. While most of the studio senior management is still Jewish, the route into a writing or producing career, in either films or television, is no longer by writing jokes for Borscht Belt comedians (*see page 84*), but rather the elite East Coast universities.

FAMOUS JEWS IN SPORTS

Jews have always participated in sports in this country, on both the professional and nonprofessional level. Today Jewish Americans are players, owners, announcers, and even commissioners in various sports.

In the early years of basketball, Jewish teams, like the Philadelphia Hebrews and the Cleveland Rosenblums, were among the stars of the (segre-gated) show. The game arose in the deprived areas of the big cities, where the Jews were living along-side other immigrant groups as well as African Americans. Playing basketball was one route to a better life. "It was absolutely a way out of the ghetto," said Dave Dabrow, one of the stars of the SPAs, the South Philadelphia Hebrew Association team. In the pre-NBA basketball scene, the SPAs stole the show: in 22 seasons, they played in 18 championship series, losing only five, and

LEFT: *Hank Greenberg hits a third-inning home run for the Phillies in a 1947 game against the Blue Jays.*

RIGHT: *Pitcher Sandy Koufax goes through his motions on the mound en route to winning the deciding game of the 1965 World Series for the Dodgers.*

their games against the Rens (The Harlem Renaissance), one of the best African-American teams, have gone down in basketball history.

Hank Greenberg (1911–1986) was the first Jewish ballplayer ever to be elected to the Hall of Fame (in 1956). The legendary first baseman once hit 58 homers in a season, and in another, drove in 183 runs (second-highest in American League history, after Lou Gehrig's 184). He was one of the greatest right-handed sluggers in the history of the game. When he did not play on Yom Kippur, it was national news. After

his playing career, he became the general manager of the Cleveland Indians, and then a part-owner of the Chicago White Sox.

Another Jewish baseball player, Brooklyn-born star pitcher Sandy Koufax, also made the news, this time in 1965, when he refused to pitch for his team, the Dodgers, in the first game of the World Series against the Minnesota Twins, because it was on Yom Kippur (he went to synagogue instead). The nation was shocked—but his stand was all but forgotten when he won the fifth and seventh games, giving the Dodgers the series.

New Immigrants

At the same time, the story of Jewish immigration is not over. The beginning of a new century and millennium has found the Jewish-American community at a crossroads in its history. Demographically, the community is going through changes. The Jewish population, formerly shrinking because of intermarriage, is being invigorated by newcomers not only from the former Soviet Union, but also from communities from the Middle and Near East and South America. In 1990, 200,000 Jews were allowed to leave the former Soviet Union, and most of them emigrated to the United States. This is a figure comparable to the earlier turn-of-the-century tidal wave of East European emigration.

Moving to America was and still is a complicated process for Russian Jews. First, they must travel to HIAS headquarters in Vienna, where they must decide between Israel and the United States as their final destination. Those who choose the United States then travel to Rome where they are housed, sheltered, and offered English classes while their papers are being processed. Of his stay in Rome, a middle-aged Russian Jew said, "In Rome we got our first taste of the West. It was beautiful. Not only the history, which was, of course, interesting to us, but the clothes, the food....For three months we celebrated." After processing is

ABOVE: *A Russian tailor takes in a dress in her shop in Brighton Beach, Brooklyn (top), and two young, Russian immigrants enjoy a night out in a Brighton Beach nightclub.*

completed, the Jews fly to New York. The Russian
Jews have formed flourishing communities in the
New York City area, most notably in the Brighton
Beach area in Brooklyn. There are also Bukharan
and Syrian Jews in Queens, New York; and Iranian
Jews in Los Angeles, as well as populations of
Israelis in most major cities in the country.

LEFT: *On the Brighton Beach boardwalk, newly arrived Russian-Jewish immigrants mingle with elderly Jews who made the same journey to America a generation earlier.*

BELOW: *Russian Jews have settled in Brighton Beach and Coney Island, where they have reinvigorated a longstanding Jewish neighborhood.*

1910 Jewish population of Lower East Side is 500,000.

1911 One quarter of Manhattan's residents are Jewish.

1911 Triangle Shirtwaist Company fire kills 146.

1914 Amalgamated Clothing Workers of America formed.

1914 The original Grossinger's in the Catskills is acquired. The family starts taking in boarders.

1915 Arthur Miller born in New York City.

1916 Louis Brandeis becomes first Jew named to the Supreme Court.

1918 Jewish population of Chicago reaches 200,000.

1924 George Gershwin composes *"Rhapsody in Blue."*

1925 Edna Ferber is first American Jew to win the Pulitzer Prize.

1928 Arnold Rothstein murdered in New York.

1930 Number of kosher butchers in New York reaches 7,500.

1934 Albert Einstein arrives in the United States.

1935 Woody Allen born in Brooklyn.

1944 Louis "Lepke" Buchalter, head of Murder Inc., executed in Sing Sing.

1947 The Displaced Persons Act brings the first of some 100,000 Holocaust survivors to America, about half Hasidim.

1948 State of Israel is created.

1949 Arthur Miller's *Death of a Salesman* is produced.

1950 Los Angeles has become second largest Jewish community in America.

LEFT: *Albert Einstein settled permanently in America after the Nazi government stripped him of his German citizenship in 1934.*

LEFT: *Bob Dylan, the grandchild of Jewish-Russian immigrants.*

1953 Julius and Ethel Rosenberg are executed as communist spies. They were convicted of giving the Soviet Union atomic secrets.

1954 Jonas Salk's polio vaccine released.

1955 Albert Einstein dies.

1956 Hank Greenberg becomes the first Jewish player named to the Baseball Hall of Fame.

1963 Elie Wiesel, novelist and spokesman for Holocaust survivors, becomes an American citizen.

1965 Los Angeles Dodger pitcher Sandy Koufax refuses to pitch in the World Series on Yom Kippur.

1967 Israel defeats its neighbors in the Six Day War.

1969 Philip Roth writes *Portnoy's Complaint.*

1973 Henry Kissinger receives Nobel Peace Prize.

1976 Saul Bellow is awarded both the Pulitzer and Nobel Prizes.

1978 Isaac Bashevis Singer wins Nobel Prize for Literature.

1980 Miami's Jewish population is more than 250,000.

1986 Elie Wiesel awarded Nobel Peace Prize.

1987 Alan Greenspan becomes head of the Federal Reserve Board.

1989 Irving Berlin dies.

1990 Russia allows 200,000 Jews to emigrate; most come to America.

1993 Ruth Bader Ginsburg is nominated to the Supreme Court.

2000 Joseph Lieberman is nominated to run for vice-president of the United States.

ABOVE: *Henry Kissinger, U.S. statesman.*

FURTHER RESOURCES

PLACES OF INTEREST

Jewish Museum of New York: a museum dedicated to Jewish life past and present around the world.

YIVO: the YIVO Jewish Institute originated in Vilna in 1925 but was moved to New York during World War II to protect its precious manuscripts and books. The library contains 3 million photographs, letters, and documents.

Tenement Museum: this museum preserves an authentic tenement along with the artifacts of the Jewish families that occupied this and similar buildings. On Sundays there are plays and slide shows dramatizing the immigrant tenement experience. The museum is run by the Lower East Side Conservancy, which strives to make it a "truly living experience."

There are other Jewish museums in 21 states and the District of Columbia. A complete list can be found on the web site of the National Museum of American Jewish History.

SYNAGOGUES

Today, it's hard to believe that literally thousands of houses of worship thrived in the Lower East Side. However, there are still a few standing and even functioning synagogues in the neighborhood.

Shaarey Shimoyim, The First American Rumanian Congregation once sat up to 1600 in its congregation

Bet Hamedrosh Hagodol Synagogue. Up until 1852, this was a Baptist Church.

The Touro Synagogue in Newport, Rhode Island, inaugurated in 1763, making it the oldest Jewish house of worship in the United States. It has been declared a national landmark.

Bet Shalom Synagogue in Elkins Park, Pennsylvania, was designed by Frank Lloyd Wright in 1954.

Spanish Portuguese Cemeteries There are three cemeteries from the Spanish-Portuguese Synagogue, Shearith Israel, in lower Manhattan. The first is located at St. James Place in Chinatown. It dates back to 1683. The other two are located on West 11th and 21st Streets.

BOOKS OF INTEREST

A History of Jews in America by H.M. Sachar (1992) Alfred A. Knopf—the title says it all, an excellent comprehensive and readable reference source

Assimilation and Its Discontents by Barry Ruben (1995) Random House—an insightful and in depth analysis of how Jews have adapted to their surroundings

Ethnic New York: A Complete Guide to the Many Faces and Cultures of New York by Mark Leeds (1991) Passport Books—one for the tourist, but informative nonetheless

Lower East Side Memories: A Jewish Place in America by Hasia R. Diner (2000) Princeton University Press—the author

is one of the foremost historians on immigrants in
the United States

Our Gang 1900–1940 by Jenna Weismann Joselit (1983)
Indiana Press—a much more comprehensive study on
Jewish Americans and crime, The author is one of the
foremost experts on Jewish-American culture

The Catskills: From Wilderness to Woodstock by Alf Evers (1972)
Doubleday & Co.—probably the most complete his-
tory of the Catskills. Evers writes extensively on
Jewish migration to the "Borscht Belt"

The Promised Land by Mary Antin (1940, reprinted 2001)
Princeton Review—the author's autobiography
describing her life, starting in Russia and her migrat-
ing to Boston.

The Uprooted by Oscar Handlin (1951, 1973) Little, Brown
and Company—about the great migrations to America.
Handlin has won the Pulitzer Prize for History

The Wonders of America: Reinventing Jewish Culture, 1880–1950
by Jenna Weismann Joselit (1994) Hill and Wang—a
wide-ranging social history of Jewish Americans during this period of time

Tough Jews, Fathers, Sons, and Gangsters by R. Cohen (1998)
Simon and Schuster—a good read

World of Our Fathers by Irving Howe (1976) Harcourt Brace
Jovanovich—a more complete and elaborate history
of Eastern European migration to America simply does
not exist

Yiddish Land by Gérard Silvain and Henri Minczeles (1999)
Gingko Press—a great picture history of the Pale of
Settlement

FILM

**A Life Apart: Hasidism in America, A History of the
Movement**—a documentary about the various sects of
Hasidism in New York and how they got there. The
video can be purchased from PBS

WEB SITES

Anyone with any experience on the Internet knows that
one site always links up with many more. Finding information on Jewish-American culture on the web is no exception. The following sites are guaranteed to lead you to
many more.

Hasidic news web site
www.Hasidicnews.com

Hebrew Immigrant Aid Society
www.hias.org

Jewish Communities of the World Web site
www.wjc.org.il/wjcbook?usa/index

Jewish Genealogical Society Inc. (has its own web site; it
is part of YIVO)
www.Religiousmovements.lib.virginia.edu

Jewish History Resources in New York State
www.sara.nysed/pubs/jewish/index.htm

Jewish Women's Archive
www.jwa.org

National Museum of American Jewish History
www.nmajh.org

INDEX